EASY DETROIT OUTDOORS

Reedy Press
PO Box 5131
St. Louis, MO 63139, USA
www.reedypress.com

Library of Congress Control Number: 2018945631

ISBN: 9781681061351

Printed in the United States of America
18 19 20 21 22   5 4 3 2 1

Cover (top to bottom): Photos courtesy of Amy S. Eckert; Amy S. Eckert; Pixabay; Pixabay
Color insert (in page order): Photos courtesy of Amy S. Eckert; Amy S. Eckert; Amy S. Eckert; Amy S. Eckert; Detroit City Football Club; Greenfield Village; Amy S. Eckert; Detroit Bikes; Amy S. Eckert; Amy S. Eckert; Greenfield Village; Amy S. Eckert; Amy S. Eckert

EASY DETROIT OUTDOORS

AMY S. ECKERT

REEDY PRESS

Photo courtesy of Amy S. Eckert

DEDICATION

To Bruce, who has always been
part of my life's greatest adventures.

Photo courtesy of Amy S. Eckert

CONTENTS

ON THE GROUND

FLORA AND FAUNA

FOOD AND CULTURE

FUN AND GAMES

Photo courtesy of Riverside Kayak Connection

PREFACE

What do you think of when you think of Detroit? If you're like most people, you picture a city hard at work manufacturing automobiles or shipping America's freight through the Detroit River. Maybe you conjure up Detroit's creative side, a music scene that ranges from Stevie Wonder to Jack White and an artistic flare encompassing the Detroit Institute of Arts and the vibrant murals of Eastern Market. Maybe these days you think of the city's rebirth, of indie restaurants, and Little Caesars Arena. I covered these attractions and more like them in *100 Things to Do in Detroit Before You Die*.

But there is also a decidedly green side to Michigan's largest city, and my goal in writing *Easy Detroit Outdoors* is to uncover this seldom-recognized side of my birthplace.

Detroiters have always loved outdoor adventures. In the 1830s, when Woodward Avenue was just a muddy road, the Detroit Boat Club Crew had already formed as a competitive rowing organization. In the 1920s, when the nation was going mad for her husband's automobiles, Clara Ford was digging in the soil, perfecting her garden at Fair Lane in Dearborn. In the 1950s, when Detroit's World War II-era vets were launching new lives in the Motor City, Mies van der Rohe was designing Lafayette Plaisance for their evening strolls, and Anna Scripps Whitcomb was transforming the Belle Isle Conservatory with six hundred orchids to improve the city's favorite greenspace for all Detroiters.

Even in the midst of one of America's great urban comeback stories modern Detroit has incorporated outdoor recreation in its plans. The Detroit RiverWalk has transformed downtown into one of the city's most beloved greenspaces and the Detroit River into a favorite paddling destination. The Outdoor Adventure Center teaches urban dwellers how to camp, compost, and kayak on the weekends, and Detroit Bikes has joined the Motor City's two-wheeled revolution, manufacturing high-quality, American-made bicycles at affordable prices.

Consider *Easy Detroit Outdoors* a glimpse of the city's natural attractions. Whether you live in Detroit or you're a newcomer discovering the joys of The D for the first time, I encourage you to explore this great American city's history and culture, its art, and its music. I also encourage you to head outside and join in a centuries-long tradition of outdoor adventures in Detroit. There is much to see in Detroit, and much of it lies outdoors.

Welcome to Detroit!
Amy S. Eckert

MICHIGAN RECREATION PASSPORT

Access to Michigan's 103 state parks and recreation areas, 138 state forest campgrounds, and fee-based boat launches is via the Michigan Recreation Passport. Residents of Michigan may purchase the passport for an annual fee of $11 when they renew their license plates or in person at any staffed Michigan state park or recreation area for $16. Non-residents of Michigan may purchase a Recreation Passport online or in person for $9/day or $32/year. Visit www.Michigan.gov/RecreationPassport for more details.

ACKNOWLEDGMENTS

A big thank you to Renee Monforton, Deanna Majchrzak, and the entire staff of the Detroit Metro Convention & Visitors Bureau. Every question I have, you answer. Every new Detroit attraction that opens, you make sure I know about it. I couldn't do what I do without you.

Photo courtesy of Amy S. Eckert

ON THE WATER

1 LEARN TO ROW WITH THE NATION'S OLDEST ROWING CLUB

In early 1839, when Detroit was still a town of only eight thousand and Woodward Avenue merely a mud road lit by candle- and lamplight, the Detroit Boat Club Crew met for the first time. That group continues to flourish to this day, making it the oldest rowing club in North America and one of the oldest continuously operating rowing organizations in the world. The Belle Isle-based boat club crew is headquartered in an elaborate stucco and terra-cotta building dating from 1902. It's great fun to watch Detroit's nationally ranked crew rowing up the Detroit River, the fluid motions of their bodies moving in perfect synchronization, but if you're interested in learning the sport yourself, you can sign up for introductory rowing classes. The Detroit Boat Club Crew offers instruction for all ages—classes for first-timers, recreational rowing for those with some experience, masters and collegiate rowing classes for those who want to perfect their skills, youth learn-to-row summer camps for sixth through twelfth grades, and junior rowing racing teams.

2 Inselruhe Ave., Detroit
313-821-9844 detroitboatclubcrew.com

KID-FRIENDLY: Yes
DOG-FRIENDLY: No
HANDICAPPED ACCESSIBLE: No
SEASON: April through October
HOURS: Classes start from 7:00 a.m. to 8:00 p.m.
COST FOR CLASSES: Adults, $275 per session; youth, $300 per session
EQUIPMENT NEEDED: Clothes that can get wet

2 CRUISE THE DETROIT RIVER WITH *DIAMOND JACK*

Since 1991 Captain Bill Hoey, a Detroit native, has transported visitors up and down the Detroit River for scenic tours of this international waterway. Two-hour tours aboard the *Diamond Jack*—formerly a Mackinac Island ferry—take cruisers past highlights of Detroit's sparkling skyline to the north and of Windsor, Canada, to the south. The trip is accompanied by historical narration that provides some background to each city. Besides public tours aboard the *Diamond Jack*, the company offers charter cruises on two other boats, the *Diamond Queen* and the *Diamond Belle,* popular for corporate parties, weddings, family reunions, and the like. Interested in venturing out a little farther into this corner of the Great Lakes? *Diamond Jack*'s River Tours offer longer cruises to Port Huron, Michigan; Toledo, Ohio; and Sans Souci and Wallaceburg, Ontario, each summer. Sight-seeing tours depart from two metro Detroit docks, one downtown and the other in Wyandotte's Bishop Park.

Detroit dock: 1340 Atwater St., Detroit
Wyandotte dock: 2701 Van Alstyne St., Wyandotte
313-843-9376 diamondjack.com

KID-FRIENDLY: Yes

DOG-FRIENDLY: No

HANDICAPPED ACCESSIBLE: Yes

SEASON: May through October

HOURS: Monday through Friday 9:00 a.m. to 5:00 p.m.

COST: Adult, $20; seniors (over 60), $18; children (5-12), $15; children 4 and under ride for free when accompanied by an adult

EQUIPMENT NEEDED: Sunglasses and sunblock

3 INVENT A NEW FISH TALE AT BISHOP PARK

Downriver from Detroit, Bishop Park hugs the Detroit River and promises anglers a nice spot for catching a big one. At dusk and again at dawn, fishing enthusiasts head to the park's large fishing pier in downtown Wyandotte with rods and reels in hand, going after walleye, yellow perch, and northern pike in spring and small- and largemouth bass and muskies in the summer. Wyandotte's annual Children's Fishing Derby and Expo takes place at this park each year, making the destination especially popular for families with young anglers, but with its variety of amenities any lovers of the outdoors will enjoy visiting. The park covers twelve acres and includes a playground, concession stand, and basketball courts as well as a popular annual fireworks show and summertime waterfront concerts. The picnic facilities are tough to beat anywhere in metro Detroit, with a spacious wooden deck, umbrellas, picnic tables, and two first-come, first-served picnic shelters. *Diamond Jack's* River Tours also have a dock in Bishop Park.

Van Alstyne St. at Vinewood St., Wyandotte
734-324-4500 wyandotte.net

KID-FRIENDLY: Yes

DOG-FRIENDLY: No

HANDICAPPED ACCESSIBLE: Limited

SEASON: Year-round

HOURS: Dawn until dusk

COST: Free

EQUIPMENT NEEDED: Fishing gear and tackle

4 TAKE THE PLUNGE FOR SPECIAL OLYMPICS

Across Michigan, supporters of the Special Olympics show their backing—and their nerve—by plunging into the frigid waters of lakes and swimming pools just as winter temperatures reach their coldest. Since its inception in 1968, Special Olympics has provided sports training and athletic competition for children and adults with physical and intellectual disabilities. Michigan has been a part of that national organization from the very beginning. The Special Olympics' annual Polar Plunge raises critical funds and awareness of the organization. Participants agree to make a financial contribution to Special Olympics (minimum contribution levels vary with location) and then take a chilly dip: Across Michigan, you can choose from twenty-eight plunges. In the Detroit area, Polar Plunges have recently taken place at the Belle Isle Boathouse, the St. Clair Boat Harbor, the Detroit Winter Blast Festival, and Rochester Mills Brewing Company. Many locations include a costume parade, a costume contest, and an After Splash Bash.

somi.org

KID-FRIENDLY: Yes

DOG-FRIENDLY: Varies with location

HANDICAPPED ACCESSIBLE: Varies with location

SEASON: January through March

HOURS: Varies with locationn

COST: The event is volunteer and donation based.

EQUIPMENT NEEDED: A crazy costume and some grit

5 LEARN TO SAIL ON LAKE ST. CLAIR

For more than twenty-five years, Lake St. Clair Sailing School has provided instruction in how to become an ASA-certified sailor and has helped already-certified sailors improve their skills. Students learn how to properly maneuver a sailboat and gain the navigational know-how necessary for wayfinding in both coastal and inland waters. Connected to Lake Huron by way of the St. Clair River and to Lake Erie by way of the Detroit River, Lake St. Clair might be thought of as a minor Great Lake, making this location a great launch pad for extensive sailing excursions. Lake St. Clair Sailing School offers classes for all abilities, from intro to sailing to skills improvement; from navigating using high-tech gear to wayfinding by means of the stars; from sailboat racing to sailing the open waters of the Great Lakes and the Caribbean, in tandem or solo. The school offers locations in St. Clair Shores and Harrison Township.

St. Clair Shores: Emerald City Harbor
24200 Jefferson Ave., St. Clair Shores

Harrison Township: Markley Marine
31300 N. River Rd., Harrison Twp.

586-770-2518 lakestclairsailingschool.com

KID-FRIENDLY: No

DOG-FRIENDLY: No

HANDICAPPED ACCESSIBLE: No

SEASON: May through October

HOURS: 9:00 a.m. to 5:00 p.m.

COSTS: $395–$795 for classes

EQUIPMENT NEEDED: Sunglasses and sunblock

6 TAKE A DIP IN THE DETROIT RIVER

Not too many years ago the notion of swimming in the Detroit River would have sent shudders down the spine of any responsible parent, but much has changed in The D since those days. Just like the city itself, the Detroit River has been beautifully cleaned up. Belle Isle has long been a beloved green respite for Detroit's urban dwellers, offering a small zoo, fountains, picnic areas, a Great Lakes museum, an aquarium, and, on hot days, a cool breeze. When temperatures really soar, though, it is the half-mile sandy Belle Isle Beach on the island's northern shore that draws crowds. The strand ranks as one of Detroiters' favorite urban swimming spots, the only public beach within Detroit's city limits or anywhere on the Detroit River. Snacks and beach chair and umbrella rentals are available. Because Belle Isle is a Michigan state park, an entrance fee is required to access the island.

2 Inselruhe Ave., Detroit
313-821-9844 belleisleconservancy.org

KID-FRIENDLY: Yes

DOG-FRIENDLY: Yes

HANDICAPPED ACCESSIBLE: Yes

SEASON: June through Labor Day

HOURS: 5:00 a.m. to 10:00 p.m. or at the conclusion of a special event

COST: Free

EQUIPMENT NEEDED: Swimming gear, sun block, and good walking shoes to explore

SPECIAL COMMENTS: A recreation passport is required, see page xiv.

7 CRUISE IN STYLE ABOARD THE *INFINITY* AND *OVATION*

The luxury yachts *Infinity* and *Ovation* bring Detroit River cruising to a new level. Launched in the 1990s, the two ships take in all of the most popular river sights: the Ambassador Bridge to Canada, Ontario's Peche Island and Detroit's Belle Isle, the Edsel and Eleanor Ford House, and the Detroit RiverWalk. The smaller of the two yachts, the 117-foot *Infinity*, is decorated with bamboo and stainless steel trimmings and accommodates 130 guests, while the 138-foot *Ovation* is paneled with dark wood. Both ships provide an on-board kitchen, a dining salon, a full-service bar and lounge, and spacious, open-air sundecks. The *Ovation* also includes meeting space and a dance floor. While the *Infinity* and the *Ovation* are frequently booked for private functions, the *Ovation* also offers the public a popular Summer Cruise Series. Summer sailings follow a theme—Uptown Jazz, Reggae on the River, or the wine-themed Continents Uncorked, for example—and include live music, dinner, and a premium open bar.

St. Clair Shores dock: Jefferson Beach Marina
24400 Jefferson Ave., St. Clair Shores
Detroit dock: 130 E. Atwater St., Detroit
586-217-3963 infinityandovation.com

KID-FRIENDLY: No

DOG-FRIENDLY: No

HANDICAPPED ACCESSIBLE: Yes

SEASON: March through December

HOURS: Monday through Friday 8:30 a.m. to 5:00 p.m.

COST: Summer Cruise Series tickets start at $105

EQUIPMENT NEEDED: A camera to preserve your memories

8 SET SAIL FOR CANADA ABOARD THE *DETROIT PRINCESS*

In her former life, the *Detroit Princess* served as a Mississippi River gambling boat in Illinois and Louisiana, and when the riverboat was eventually replaced by a larger vessel, there was talk of scrapping the ship. Instead, CJC Cruises purchased and remodeled the boat, adding a full kitchen and restaurant and outfitting her for sightseeing cruises. Since 2005, the Detroit Princess has been docked alongside Hart Plaza in the center of downtown, carrying sightseers up and down the Detroit River for photo-worthy views of the Detroit RiverWalk to the north and the Windsor skyline to the south. Spanning 222 feet in length, the ship has five decks (including large outdoor viewing areas on the upper two floors) and can carry as many as fifteen hundred passengers. Cruises include Motown-themed lunch and dinner cruises, floating beer tastings, fireworks sailings scheduled around Canada's and America's respective Independence Days (July 1 and 4), and winter holiday parties. Private charters are also available.

Dock: Hart Plaza, Atwater St. at Civic Center Dr., Detroit
877-DET-BOAT (877-338-2628)
detroitprincess.com

KID-FRIENDLY: Yes, depending upon cruise theme

DOG-FRIENDLY: No

HANDICAPPED ACCESSIBLE: Yes

SEASON: March through December

HOURS: Monday through Friday 9:00 a.m. to 5:00 p.m.

COST: Prices vary. $24–$58

EQUIPMENT NEEDED: Sunglasses and sunblock

9 EXPLORE DETROIT'S WATERWAYS WITH SUP

In a noisy urban center like Detroit's, standup paddleboarding offers a quiet alternative for exercise and relaxation. SUP has exploded in popularity nationally over the past decade. That's true in the Motor City, too, and little surprise. Few American cities offer greater access to paddle-worthy waters, and statewide Michigan is home to some three thousand miles of water trails. Outfitters across the city—most of them centered on the Detroit River and Lake St. Clair—provide the gear and know-how to navigate Detroit's waters with SUP. Favorite standup destinations include Detroit's historic canals just east of Belle Isle; the calm surfaces of Lake Muscoday and Blue Heron Lagoon on Belle Isle; Lake St. Clair and its surrounding parks; and even the Detroit River, depending upon weather and your skill level. There's even an annual SUP Sprint and Splash race at Lake St. Clair Metropark. Although die-hard standup paddlers venture onto Detroit's waters year-round, the city's chilly waters limit most SUP enthusiasts to the summer.

Belle Isle Park: Rentals
2 Inselruhe Ave., Detroit
313-821-9844, belleisleconservancy.org

Detroit River Sports: Rentals, tours
Fisherman's Marina
14601 Riverside Blvd., Detroit
313-908-0484, detroitriversports.com

Great Lakes Surf Shop: Classes, rentals
23517 Nine Mack Dr. Suite B,
St. Clair Shores
586-359-6961, greatlakessurf.com

Riverside Kayak Connection: Classes, rentals
4016 Biddle Ave., Wyandotte
734-285-2925, riversidekayak.com

KID-FRIENDLY: Yes

DOG-FRIENDLY: Varies with location

HANDICAPPED ACCESSIBLE: Limited

SEASON: May through September

HOURS: Varies per location

COST: Varies per location

EQUIPMENT NEEDED: Sunglasses and sunblock

10 FISH FOR BASS, WALLEYE, AND MUSKIE WITH A FISHING CHARTER

The waterways surrounding Detroit—Lake Huron, Lake Erie, Lake St. Clair, and the St. Clair and Detroit Rivers—are a boat fisherman's dream. While fish species vary from one body of water to another, you can count on finding ample small- and largemouth bass, perch, pike, walleye, steelhead, and muskie, depending on the season. A Detroit-based fishing charter helps take the guesswork out of where to fish and when. Knowledgeable about which fish are in season and likely to be biting, intimately familiar with tried-and-true fishing spots in Detroit and Lake St. Clair, and loaded with first-rate equipment, lures, bait, and licenses, metro Detroit's fishing charters mark the surest way to a good day on the water. If you're new to angling, you'll ramp up your skills alongside an experienced charter fisherman. Departure points vary with the season and the desired catch. Some charters also provide fish-cleaning services at trip's end.

Great Lakes Bass Fishing
313-319-0100
greatlakesbassfishing.com

Miller's Sportfishing Charters
734-395-8820
millers-sportfishing.com

Muskie Mania Sportfishing Charters
586-260-4068
muskiemaniacharters.com

Walleye 101
810-965-3960
walleye101.com

KID-FRIENDLY: Yes

DOG-FRIENDLY: Varies with outfitter

HANDICAPPED ACCESSIBLE: Varies with outfitter

SEASON: Spring through autumn

HOURS: Depends on charter booked

COST: Depends on charter booked

EQUIPMENT NEEDED: Your imagination, the better to craft a good fish tale

11 DISCOVER HISTORIC CANALS WITH RIVERSIDE KAYAK CONNECTION

Sometimes referred to as "Detroit's Little Venice," the narrow canals that slice into the city's eastern neighborhoods offer a glimpse of Detroit seldom seen, and they are views best seen from the water. Riverside Kayak Connection guides paddlers up the Detroit River, in and out of several of these canals, offering a look at such places as the Fisher Mansion and hangouts once frequented by the Purple Gang, a band of notorious Prohibition-era bootleggers. The Historical Canal Tour is just one outing organized by the Riverside Kayak Connection. Other tours circumnavigate Belle Isle and Grosse Ile; explore the Detroit River at sunset or during a full moon; paddle the River Rouge or the Detroit River as far as Wyandotte; and explore the Humbug Marsh, the last remaining natural shoreline on the American side of the Detroit River. Paddling tours may be booked with or without rental of a kayak, and departure points vary with the tour. Riverside Kayak Connection also has a location on Belle Isle.

4016 Biddle Ave., Wyandotte
734-285-2925 riversidekayak.com

KID-FRIENDLY: Yes

DOG-FRIENDLY: No

HANDICAPPED ACCESSIBLE: Limited

SEASON: May through October

HOURS: MTuWF 10:00 a.m. to 6:00 p.m.; Thurs. 10:00 a.m. to 7:00 p.m.; Sat. 10:00 a.m. to 4:00 p.m.; Sun. 12–4:00 p.m.

COST: Varies; $25–$30 without kayak rental; $40–$50 with kayak rental

EQUIPMENT NEEDED: Sunblock and a sense of curiosity

12 EXPLORE LAKE ST. CLAIR WITH THE DETROIT OUTPOST

The female-owned kayak touring company Detroit Outpost puts visitors at water level with Lake St. Clair and offers an opportunity to see just how close you can get to lumbering Great Lakes freighters, fishing boats, and sleek sailboats on the Detroit River. Of special interest is the Nautical Mile, a popular district of destination restaurants and independently owned shops in St. Clair Shores. Lake St. Clair, connected to Lake Huron by way of the St. Clair River and to Lake Erie by way of the Detroit River, might be thought of as a tiny Great Lake in its own right. The guides at Detroit Outpost share the history of these important waterways, explain The D's long maritime past, and offer tales of the outrageous Purple Gang, a dangerous band of bootleggers from Detroit's Prohibition days. Excursions begin near the Detroit Outpost's shop, on the mainland near the eastern end of Belle Isle.

Riverside Marina, 11000 Freud St., Detroit
313-422-3618 detroitoutpost.com

KID-FRIENDLY: Yes. Children under age 12 must ride with an adult

DOG-FRIENDLY: No

HANDICAPPED ACCESSIBLE: Limited

SEASON: May through October

HOURS: Monday, Wednesday, Friday, 10:00 a.m. to 3:00 p.m.

COST: $40

EQUIPMENT NEEDED: Sunglasses and sunblock

13 COOL OFF WITH A SWIM AT LAKE ST. CLAIR

When the mercury soars, there's no better place to cool off than the Lake St. Clair Metropark. Set on a little spit of land that reaches into Lake St. Clair, this Metropark sits six miles east of Mt. Clemens. In summer, the park's one-thousand-foot sandy beach fills with families swimming, sunbathing, and building sandcastles, but there's also an Olympic-size outdoor swimming pool with spectacular water slides, an inflatable floating obstacle course, and climbing walls. If that's not enough to keep the family chill on a hot summer day, you can always head to the Squirt Zone Spray Ground with its squirting in-ground fountains and water cannons. Lake St. Clair Metropark offers a wide range of activities after the children have become sufficiently water-logged: mini golf, hiking trails, boat and bike rentals, fishing, and, in winter, cross-country skiing. Lifeguards are stationed at the swimming pool only. A bathhouse and concessions are located near the pool.

31300 Metro Parkway, Harrison Twp.
586-463-4581 metroparks.com

KID-FRIENDLY: Yes

DOG-FRIENDLY: No

HANDICAPPED ACCESSIBLE: Limited

SEASON: Park, year-round; pools, Memorial Day through Labor Day; beach, May through September

HOURS: 6:00 a.m. to 10:00 p.m.

COST: Free

EQUIPMENT NEEDED: Sunglasses and sunblock

14 PADDLE AROUND BELLE ISLE

Belle Isle has long been a green oasis for Detroiters, a quiet respite with a small zoo, a Great Lakes museum, fountains, an aquarium, picnic areas, and a swimming beach. In 2014 the state of Michigan acquired Belle Isle as its 102nd state park, a move that allowed for some major park infrastructure improvements. Small craft boat launches, one at Belle Isle Beach and another at Flynn Pavilion, were part of that grand redevelopment as were canoe and kayak rentals and guided tours, also at Flynn Pavilion. Paddlers can make their way around the island, sharing space with the Great Lakes freighters that ply these waters, or paddle the island's Blue Heron Lagoon for picture-postcard views of Detroit's sparkling skyline, the towers of GM's Renaissance Center standing front and center. Other highlights include views of the Windsor riverfront to the south and Milliken State Park's wetlands and lighthouse on the Detroit shore. Because Belle Isle is now a state park, an entrance fee is required to access the island.

2 Inselruhe Ave., Detroit
313-821-9844 belleisleconservancy.org

KID-FRIENDLY: Yes, all ages

DOG-FRIENDLY: Yes

HANDICAPPED ACCESSIBLE: Yes

SEASON: April through September

HOURS: 5:00 a.m. to 10:00 p.m. or at the conclusion of a special event

COST: Free with your own boat; canoes, pedal boats, tandem kayaks and SUP $15/hr.; solo kayaks $10/hr.

EQUIPMENT NEEDED: Sunglasses, sunblock, and a boat

SPECIAL COMMENTS: A recreation passport is required, see page xiv.

15 PADDLE TO DINNER WITH DETROIT RIVER SPORTS

What's better than spending an evening paddling the Detroit skyline? How about satisfying the appetite you just worked up with a tasty dinner grown right in Detroit? Detroit River Sports guides kayakers from its location at Fisherman's Marina, a once-abandoned marina on Detroit's far-east side now brimming with activity since its reopening in 2017. Paddlers explore the Detroit River, working their way past Belle Isle, into eastern Detroit's historic canals and within sight of Windsor, Canada, to the south. The evening wraps up with dinner at Coriander Kitchen and Farm, a locally sourced restaurant set within the marina. Detroit River Sports offers a variety of additional tours, including food-free excursions, kayaking Detroit by the light of a full moon, and standup paddling tours of the river, the historic canals of Detroit, and nearby Lake St. Clair. Paddlers with their own kayaks and boards are welcome to use Detroit River Sports' launch for solo excursions free of charge.

14601 Riverside Blvd., Detroit
313-908-0484 detroitriversports.com

KID-FRIENDLY: Yes. Children under age 12 ride with an adult

DOG-FRIENDLY: No

HANDICAPPED ACCESSIBLE: Limited

SEASON: May through October

HOURS: Arrive at 5:00 p.m. for Paddle to Table

COST: Paddle to Table from $80

EQUIPMENT NEEDED: Walking shoes for an after-dinner stroll along the Detroit RiverWalk

16 COMBINE CRUISING WITH BEER TASTING ON A MOTOR CITY BREW TOUR

Stephen Johnson and Motor City Brew Tours have since 2009 guided bicyclists through Detroit on a quest to learn the city's history, to hear its sometimes bizarre stories and, naturally, to drink beer, but the outfitter headed to the water in 2012, offering Detroit River cruises that include ample beer tastings. Cruises take place aboard the *Detroit Princess*, once a Mississippi riverboat that was refitted and transported to the Motor City for river cruising in 2005. On board, visitors see the sparkling Detroit and Windsor skylines and all of the river's most popular landmarks: the Ambassador Bridge to Canada, Belle Isle and Milliken State Parks, and the Detroit RiverWalk. They also enjoy appetizers and drink samples from a lineup of thirty craft beers and hard ciders, some brewed right in Detroit and others from farther afield. Motor City Brew Tours typically offers three sailings per year: Father's Day, featuring spring beers; a summer beer tasting; and an autumn-themed Boatoberfest in October.

Dock: Hart Plaza, Atwater St. at Civic Center Dr., Detroit
248-825-3085 motorcitybrewtours.com

KID-FRIENDLY: No

DOG-FRIENDLY: No

HANDICAPPED ACCESSIBLE: Yes

SEASON: Spring, summer, and autumn

HOURS: 9:00 a.m. to 5:00 p.m.

COST: Bike and brew tours, $10–$35

EQUIPMENT NEEDED: Sunglasses and your wallet . . . in case one beer is not enough

17 PEDAL AND PARTY ON A DETROIT CYCLE BOAT

Michigan's first cycle boat launched on the banks of the Detroit River in 2017. Combining exercise, a Detroit River sightseeing tour, and a bar, the Detroit Cycle Boat offers partiers a good time while requiring them to work for their drinks. The party cruises depart from Sindbad's Restaurant and Marina loaded with beer, wine, liquor, a nice sound system, and all of the standard boating safety equipment. Then guests pedal out into the Detroit River for a tour of the city's beautiful riverfront. There's room on the boat to walk around and even bench seats if you need a break from pedaling. Since you can bring your own snacks and drinks on board, visitors can make a Detroit Cycle Boat experience as family friendly as they like. A flat rate gets you exclusive use of the boat for two hours. The boat has space to accommodate as few as six and as many as sixteen passengers on board.

100 St. Clair St., Detroit
231-286-5257 detroitcycleboat.com

KID-FRIENDLY: Yes

DOG-FRIENDLY: No

HANDICAPPED ACCESSIBLE: No

SEASON: Mid-May through early October

HOURS: 10:00 a.m. to 9:00 p.m.

COST: $35 per person

EQUIPMENT NEEDED: Sunglasses and sunblock

18 LEARN TO KAYAK WITH THE RIVERSIDE KAYAK CONNECTION

Detroit's proximity to the Detroit River and Lake St. Clair makes paddling sports readily available, but for many urban dwellers, kayaking is an unfamiliar pastime. Riverside Kayak Connection puts Detroit's water within reach for people of all ages and abilities. Lessons range from intro kayaking and beginner SUP to advanced boat maneuvering, kayak rolling, wet exits, water navigation, and rescues. Other classes are designed to assist paddlers with limited physical mobility and to certify paddling instructors. Once you've learned to paddle, you can put your newfound skills into practice on a guided tour. Riverside Kayak Connection leads tours that explore Detroit's historical canals, circumnavigate Grosse Ile and Belle Isle, paddle the Detroit River at sunset or full moon, and explore the Detroit River as far as Wyandotte. Paddling tours may be booked with or without rental of a kayak, and departure points vary with the tour. Riverside Kayak Connection also has a location on Belle Isle.

4016 Biddle Ave., Wyandotte
734-285-2925 riversidekayak.com

KID-FRIENDLY: Yes

DOG-FRIENDLY: No

HANDICAPPED ACCESSIBLE: Limited

SEASON: May through October

HOURS: MTuWF 10:00 a.m. to 6:00 p.m., Thurs. 10:00 a.m. to 7:00 p.m., Sat. 10:00 a.m. to 4:00 p.m., Sun. 12–4:00 p.m.

COST: Classes from $60

EQUIPMENT NEEDED: Sunglasses, sunblock, and a sense of humor

Photo courtesy of Amy S. Eckert

ON THE GROUND

19 PEDAL THE D AT SLOW ROLL

Avid bicyclists and newbies, city dwellers and suburbanites, those pedaling mountain bikes, those on cruisers, and those on custom rides tricked out with lights, bells, and sound systems, all ages and backgrounds take to Detroit's city streets by the thousands each Monday evening for a casual two-wheeled tour. Begun in 2010 by Detroiters Jason Hall and Mike MacKool, two bicycle-riding friends interested in incorporating a little exercise into their weekly meetups, Slow Roll has exploded in size and popularity. In 2017 more than ten thousand people explored Detroit on twenty-three Slow Roll rides, and the concept has taken off to include Chicago, Cleveland, Minneapolis, Washington, DC, and even Berlin and Stockholm, all of the rides patterned after an idea born in Detroit. Slow Roll departure points vary weekly, and riders are asked to register online. Membership is free, with a modest donation requested to defray the costs of police escorts and porta-potties.

slowroll.bike

KID-FRIENDLY: Yes

DOG-FRIENDLY: Yes

HANDICAPPED ACCESSIBLE: Yes

SEASON: Year-round

HOURS: Mondays with a few holiday exceptions; meet at 6:00 p.m., ride at 7:00 p.m.

COST: Free; donations accepted

EQUIPMENT NEEDED: Bicycle and helmet

20 GO SNOWBOARDING AT ALPINE VALLEY

Detroit isn't exactly mountainous, but Alpine Valley keeps area snowboarders happy just the same. The ski resort in Detroit's northwestern suburbs is typically blessed with good North Country snow in the depths of winter, but because Mother Nature can sometimes be stingy, 100 percent of the resort's runs are covered by snow equipment to ensure a long season. Alpine Valley ranks as southeastern Michigan's largest ski area and draws schussers and boarders from across this corner of the state. Four terrain parks, including a half pipe, are carved out of Alpine Valley's twelve-hundred-foot mountain, while skiers can take advantage of twenty-five tree-lined downhill ski slopes, eleven of them designed for beginners, eight for more advanced skiers, and all of them serviced by nine chair lifts and four tow ropes. Alpine Valley provides rentals and lessons for every age group as well as a number of racing programs. The ski resort's Hornet's Nest lounge offers snacks, drinks, and occasional live music.

6775 Highland Rd., White Lake
248-887-2180 skialpinevalley.com

KID-FRIENDLY: Yes

DOG-FRIENDLY: No

HANDICAPPED ACCESSIBLE: Limited

SEASON: Winter

HOURS: 9:00 a.m. to 10:00 p.m.

COST: Lift tickets start at $37; beginner hill tickets start at $30

EQUIPMENT NEEDED: Snow gear

21 ENJOY YOGA ON THE DETROIT RIVER

All summer long Detroit's Urban Solace studio offers hour-long yoga sessions on the banks of the Detroit River, surrounded by the verdant wetlands of William G. Milliken State Park. You could hardly find a more pleasant outdoor location in which to perform your warrior poses and downward dogs. Brilliant flower beds rim the edges of the state park. Working and pleasure boats travel down the Detroit River, and overhead towers the sparkling glass and steel of Detroit's most impressive downtown buildings. Urban Solace's yoga classes result from a partnership with the Detroit Riverfront Conservancy, the organization that transformed the city's once decaying waterfront into one of the nation's prettiest. Adjacent to Milliken State Park and stretching in either direction is the Detroit RiverWalk, where you can wrap up your evening with a walk past amphitheaters, a carousel, fountains, a lovely white lighthouse, and lots of good people watching. Yoga classes are free, and no registration is required. Participants should bring their own yoga mats and drinking water.

Detroit Riverfront Conservancy, Detroit
313-566-8200 detroitriverfront.org

KID-FRIENDLY: Yes

DOG-FRIENDLY: No

HANDICAPPED ACCESSIBLE: Limited

SEASON: June through August

HOURS: Classes at 6:00 p.m. Thursday and 10:00 a.m. Friday

COST: Free

EQUIPMENT NEEDED: Yoga gear and walking shoes for a post-yoga walk along the Detroit RiverWalk

SPECIAL COMMENTS: Classes held in Milliken State Park, but no recreation passport is required.

22 CYCLE THE CITY WITH WHEELHOUSE DETROIT

Detroit has gained a reputation in recent years as a city especially friendly to bicyclists, thanks in large part to the popularity of Slow Roll and the emergence of quality bike manufacturers, such as Shinola and Detroit Bikes. Wheelhouse Detroit provides access to wheels for those who would prefer to rent. Choose from a dozen bikes, from children's BMXs to hybrids and tandems, and rent from two hours to a period of weeks. Their downtown facility sits at an ideal location for heading off on a two-wheeled outing. Set right on the Detroit RiverWalk, riders can pedal the length of the 3.5-mile pathway and then veer up the Dequindre Cut for another two-mile vehicle-free ride to Eastern Market. If you're interested in riding with others—and perhaps learning a little of Detroit's history and culture—join one of twenty-three tours centered on such themes as public art, Detroit's techno scene, urban agriculture, and auto heritage. You can tour with your own bike or rent from Wheelhouse Detroit for just ten dollars more.

1340 Atwater St., Detroit, 313-656-2453
9401 Joseph Campau Ave., Hamtramck, 313-871-2811
wheelhousedetroit.com

KID-FRIENDLY: Yes

DOG-FRIENDLY: No

HANDICAPPED ACCESSIBLE: No

SEASON: April through October

HOURS: Mon.–Sat. 10:00 a.m. to 5:00 p.m.; Sun. 10:00 a.m. to 8:00 p.m.

COST: Adults from $15/2 hours

EQUIPMENT NEEDED: Sunglasses

23 RUN ALONG THE DETROIT RIVERWALK

Spanning 3.5 miles from Cobo Center toward Belle Isle, the Detroit RiverWalk links together a chain of riverfront gems: William G. Milliken State Park, Rivard Plaza, and the popular gathering place at Hart Plaza. This lovely green space is like a breath of fresh air in downtown Detroit, where just a few years ago the Detroit River lapped against an embarrassing array of abandoned parking lots and crumbling breakwaters. Today's RiverWalk includes outdoor amphitheaters, natural wetlands, a towering white lighthouse, a Great Lakes animal-themed carousel, fountains, public art, colorful flower beds, marinas, and a view of Windsor, Ontario, just across the water. The RiverWalk ranks as a favorite location for a morning run or a lunchtime stroll, and it connects with the Dequindre Cut greenway if you're inclined to extend your run or bike ride. Wheelhouse Detroit rents bikes on the RiverWalk near Atwater and Rivard Streets. Plans are to expand the RiverWalk in both directions, connecting with the Ambassador Bridge in the west and Belle Isle in the east.

Rosa Parks Blvd. to the Belle Isle Bridge, Detroit
313-566-8200 detroitriverfront.org

KID-FRIENDLY: Yes

DOG-FRIENDLY: Yes, on a leash

HANDICAPPED ACCESSIBLE: Yes

SEASON: Year-round

HOURS: Detroit RiverWalk and Dequindre Cut Greenway open daily from 6:00 a.m. to 10:00 p.m.

COST: Free

EQUIPMENT NEEDED: Running shoes and sunglasses

24 WALK THROUGH AMERICAN HISTORY AT GREENFIELD VILLAGE

Henry Ford so enjoyed collecting historical artifacts and items associated with human innovation that he set aside this piece of land alongside his Dearborn estate to preserve and display his finds. Within the Henry Ford Museum of Innovation you'll find Lincoln's trademark top hat and a parade of historic vehicles, but at adjacent Greenfield Village visitors can stroll through eighty acres of noteworthy houses and buildings. Walk through Thomas Edison's Fort Meyers laboratory and his Menlo Park complex, where the scientist patented the electric light bulb, the phonograph, and some four hundred other inventions. Visit the Wright Brothers' Dayton, Ohio, bicycle shop and the homes of poet Robert Frost and dictionary author Noah Webster. Colonial-era houses from Massachusetts, Connecticut, and New Hampshire are open to walk through as is a nineteenth-century Maryland plantation. There are even a Swiss chalet and a Cotswold cottage on-site, all of the properties purchased and subsequently moved here to Henry Ford's Dearborn property. While you're visiting, take the opportunity to ride in an authentic Model T.

20900 Oakwood Blvd., Dearborn
313-982-6001 thehenryford.org

KID-FRIENDLY: Yes

DOG-FRIENDLY: No

HANDICAPPED ACCESSIBLE: Yes

SEASON: Mid-April through December

HOURS: 9:30 a.m. to 5:00 p.m.; open daily April 14 to Oct. 28; open Fri.-Sun. Oct. 29 through Nov. 26; occasional evening openings.

COST: $28 for adults, $25.50 for seniors, and $21 for youth. If you plan to visit multiple venues at The Henry Ford, save money with a package purchase.

EQUIPMENT NEEDED: Sunglasses and a camera

25 BICYCLE TO EASTERN MARKET BY THE GRAFFITI-RICH DEQUINDRE CUT GREENWAY

Once an abandoned leg of the Grand Trunk Railroad Line, the Dequindre Cut extends the pleasant green space that has made Detroit's riverfront so popular in recent years. The two-mile paved urban recreation trail is divided into pedestrian and bicycle lanes and lies largely below street grade, leading northward from the Detroit RiverWalk and the Outdoor Adventure Center to the shops, restaurants, and neighborhoods around historic Eastern Market. This path has long attracted graffiti artists, particularly back in the days when it served merely as a railroad cut. During redevelopment of the strip, a great effort was made to retain those artworks that were family appropriate and to augment with even more. Consequently, the Dequindre Cut is something of a monument to urban art as well as a multiuse path. The existing Dequindre Cut is just the beginning of a larger plan to one day expand the trail to a distance of twenty-seven miles.

Detroit RiverWalk to Gratiot Ave.
313-566-8200 detroitriverfront.org

KID-FRIENDLY: Yes

DOG-FRIENDLY: Yes

HANDICAPPED ACCESSIBLE: Yes

SEASON: Year-round

HOURS: Detroit RiverWalk and Dequindre Cut Greenway open daily from 6:00 a.m. to 10:00 p.m.

COST: Free

EQUIPMENT NEEDED: Bicycle, wallet, and a shopping basket

26 EXPLORE ARCHITECTURE WITH PRESERVATION DETROIT

When Detroit was rolling in money back in the 1920s, the city flaunted its success with grand architecture. There was the art deco Penobscot Building, the eighth-tallest building in the world when it was constructed in 1928. The Guardian Building, known as the "Cathedral of Finance" when it was built in 1929, was covered with nearly two million tangerine-colored bricks on the outside, while its interior was decorated with gold leaf and tiled in a brightly colored Mayan design. The art deco, Albert Kahn-designed Fisher Building, also constructed in 1929, originally bore a gold-plated roof. These architectural gems and others find their place on tours with Preservation Detroit, an organization devoted to sharing the city's rich cultural heritage while using its profits to preserve Detroit buildings that might otherwise fall into ruin. Two-hour tours cover the highlights of downtown, Midtown and the Cultural Center, and Eastern Market, on foot or by bicycle.

313-577-3559
preservationdetroit.org

KID-FRIENDLY: Yes

DOG-FRIENDLY: No

HANDICAPPED ACCESSIBLE: Limited

SEASON: May through September

HOURS: Mon.–Tue. 8:30 a.m. to 4:30 p.m., Wed. 8:30 a.m. to 12:30 p.m., Sat. 9:00 a.m. to noon

COST: Tour prices $12–$15

EQUIPMENT NEEDED: Sunglasses, good walking shoes, and a camera

27 RUN THE TURKEY TROT AT AMERICA'S THANKSGIVING PARADE

Since 1982 Detroiters have made a tradition of working up a pre-Thanksgiving dinner appetite by participating in the Turkey Trot. Several races are available: a 10K, a 5K, and a one-mile run/walk, all of them stroller (but not pet) friendly. The Turkey Trot is much more than merely a race. Thousands of participants join in the fun each year, making this the nation's largest Thanksgiving morning race and the largest spectator event in Michigan, and most Turkey Trotters arrive at the starting line adorned in fun costumes. "The Parade before the Parade," as the Turkey Trot is often called, takes place just hours before the start of Detroit's immensely popular America's Thanksgiving Parade, a beloved part of the city's holiday traditions since 1924. Giant helium-filled balloons, colorful floats, scores of marching bands, and a colorful Distinguished Clown Corps of more than two thousand participate in the main event, welcoming the holiday season with great fanfare. All racers receive a participant's shirt and a finisher's medal.

theparade.org

KID-FRIENDLY: Yes

DOG-FRIENDLY: No

HANDICAPPED ACCESSIBLE: Limited

SEASON: Thanksgiving Day

HOURS: Turkey Trot, 7:30 a.m.; Mashed Potato Mile, 7:30 a.m.; Stuffing Strut 5K, 8:30 a.m.

COST: 5K–10K, $39–$49; one mile, $23–$29

EQUIPMENT NEEDED: Running shoes and a goofy costume

28 BICYCLE BELLE ISLE STATE PARK

Surrounded by the Detroit River and located just four miles from downtown, Belle Isle's one thousand acres offer a quiet natural retreat for urban dwellers. Designated a Michigan state park in 2014 (you'll need to pay an entrance fee now) and accessible by the Douglas MacArthur Bridge, Belle Isle's list of pastimes ranges from picnicking within view of the Detroit skyline to the Detroit Grand Prix IndyCar races around the park's paved streets, from standup paddling Blue Heron Lagoon to cruising down a multistory slide. One of the most popular ways to see it all is by circumnavigating Belle Isle on two wheels. The easy paved route passes a small zoo and aquarium, a swimming beach, a driving range, fountains, a Great Lakes museum, Lake Muscoday, and the Livingstone Memorial Lighthouse built in 1929, the only lighthouse in the nation constructed of marble. Don't have your own bicycle with you? Rent one at Flynn Pavilion on Belle Isle or at Wheelhouse Detroit on the Detroit RiverWalk.

2 Inselruhe Ave., Detroit
313-821-9844 belleisleconservancy.org

KID-FRIENDLY: Yes

DOG-FRIENDLY: Yes

HANDICAPPED ACCESSIBLE: Yes

SEASON: Year-round, rentals from April through October

HOURS: 5:00 a.m. to 10:00 p.m., or at the conclusion of a special event

COST: Free

EQUIPMENT NEEDED: Bicycle and helmet

SPECIAL COMMENTS: A recreation passport is required, see page xiv.

29 LEARN TO CAMP, FISH, AND HUNT DOWNTOWN AT THE OUTDOOR ADVENTURE CENTER

It can be hard to appreciate Michigan's great outdoors when you live in the heart of a major urban center. Where can you try your hand at camping? How do you learn the necessary skills to fish? Enter the Outdoor Adventure Center, which replicates the very best of Michigan's many outdoor experiences: hiking state park trails, viewing northern Michigan's towering waterfalls, or operating a fishing boat or a snowmobile. Many of the OAC's exhibits are indoors, including virtual reality kayaking and boat fishing, but the center prides itself on the wide array of practical outdoor learning experiences offered. Sign up for a women-only archery class. Take a guided hike through the surrounding grasslands looking for resident ring-necked pheasants or migrating songbirds. Take a composting class or volunteer for a beach cleanup day. The classes are all aimed at whetting urban dwellers' appetite for the great outdoors—even in the midst of the city center.

1801 Atwater St., Detroit
844-622-6367 michigan.gov/oac

KID-FRIENDLY: Yes

DOG-FRIENDLY: No

HANDICAPPED ACCESSIBLE: Varies with program

SEASON: Year-round

HOURS: Wed.–Fri. 10:00 a.m. to 3:00 p.m., Sat. 10:00 a.m. to 5:00 p.m., Sun. 12:00–5:00 p.m.

COST: Adults, $5; children and seniors, $3; children under 2, free

EQUIPMENT NEEDED: Good walking shoes and a sense of discovery

SPECIAL COMMENTS: Annual family membership available for $50

30 CRUISE DETROIT BY SEGWAY

High-tech and emission free, active and fun, Detroit Segway offers an enjoyable way to get out and discover the neighborhoods of The D, and the tours are faster and easier than exploring on foot. Launched in 2007, owner Maureen Kearns sought to show off her hometown in style. The company has now expanded to include ten downtown tours. Most popular is the three-hour Whole Shebang tour that leads visitors along the Detroit RiverWalk, through Grand Circus Park, up Woodward Avenue, through Eastern Market, and along the Dequindre Cut. Other tours run closer to two hours and focus on Upper Downtown, including Comerica Park and Campus Martius; Belle Isle; or Downtown Holiday Lights, with the city all lit up for the season. Not interested in joining an organized tour? You can rent a Segway and instead head off on your own. Segways are permitted on any Detroit city sidewalks and most sections of the RiverWalk.

2934 Russell St., Detroit
855-873-4929 detroitsegway.com

KID-FRIENDLY: Age 14 and up; under 18 must be accompanied by an adult

DOG-FRIENDLY: No

HANDICAPPED ACCESSIBLE: No

SEASON: Mid-May through October

HOURS: TuWThF 11:00 a.m. to 4:00 p.m., Sat. 9:00 a.m. to 4:00 p.m., Sun. 10:00 a.m. to 4:00 p.m.

COST: 1 hour, $50; 2 hours, $100; 4 hours, $200

EQUIPMENT NEEDED: Sunglasses and good shoes

31 TAKE A HIKE (OR A BIKE) ALONG THE IRON BELLE TRAIL

When the Iron Belle Trail is finished (the trail is currently 69% complete), this route will rank as the longest designated state trail in the United States, crisscrossing Michigan from the metro Detroit area all the way to Ironwood in the state's western Upper Peninsula. The Iron Belle takes a portion of its name from the path's starting point on Belle Isle in downtown Detroit. Two distinct paths constitute the Iron Belle—the longer, more rustic path ideal for hikers and the shorter, more finely paved one for cyclists—but here in Detroit, it doesn't matter whether you prefer hiking or biking. The two paths are one and the same. Begin on Belle Isle and cross onto Michigan's mainland by the MacArthur Bridge. Then follow the Detroit RiverWalk to the Dequindre Cut and northward to Eastern Market. From there, it's a mere 1,250-odd miles by foot (approximately 770 miles by bicycle) through forty-eight Michigan counties, white pine forests, over the Mackinac Bridge, and eventually alongside the Lake Superior shore to Ironwood.

michigan.gov/dnr

KID-FRIENDLY: Yes

DOG-FRIENDLY: Yes

HANDICAPPED ACCESSIBLE: Varies by trail segment

SEASON: Year-round

HOURS: Dawn to dusk

COST: Free

EQUIPMENT NEEDED: Hiking shoes and/or a bicycle helmet

SPECIAL COMMENTS: A recreation passport is required only for the portion of the trail that crosses Belle Isle, see page xiv.

32 SEE THE MOTOR CITY SANS MOTOR WITH TOUR DE TROIT

Detroit is quickly becoming a city of cyclists. From the immensely popular Slow Roll movement to the new MoGo bike share system and locally manufactured Shinola and Detroit Bikes, two-wheeled transportation has become all the rage. Add to that list the Tour de Troit, a bike ride held annually in mid-September that is less a race than a group cycle fest. Participants can register for the Main Tour de Troit, a 25.6-mile leisurely ride across the city with police escort and three mechanic pit stops or the Metric Tour de Troit, a one-hundred-kilometer (sixty-two-mile) non-escorted ride for very experienced cyclists. Although these races mark the year's big events for organizers, the Tour de Troit team offers additional bicycle-themed events throughout the year, including the Martin Luther King, Jr., Memorial Ride; the Rouge-a-Thlon duathlon at Rouge Park; Bike the Bridge, a rare opportunity to cycle to Canada and back by the Ambassador Bridge; the Tour d'Eastside from the Detroit River to Eight Mile; and the Paczki Run 5K foot race.

tour-de-troit.org

KID-FRIENDLY: Yes

DOG-FRIENDLY: No

HANDICAPPED ACCESSIBLE: No

SEASON: Events year-round; Tour de Troit takes place each September.

HOURS: Main ride starts at 9:00 a.m.

COST: Varies with event, from free to $40-$60 for the Tour de Troit

EQUIPMENT NEEDED: Bicycle and helmet

33 EXPLORE ABANDONED DETROIT ON A MOTOR CITY PHOTOGRAPHY TOUR

In spite of Detroit's much-heralded renaissance, much remains of the abandoned city so much in the news just a few short years ago. Head to the right corner of town and you'll still find idle automotive factories left in ruins and decorated with graffiti, elaborate estates abandoned to decay when the city's population left for the suburbs, cityscapes marked with fallow fields, and asphalt choked by knee-high weeds and saplings, all evidence of a municipal budget too depleted to maintain its infrastructure. Many visitors to Detroit remain fascinated by the abandonment and even the beauty of these deteriorating sights. Photographer Jesse Welter is one of these people. He founded Motor City Photography Workshops in 2011 to guide other curious types to Detroit's most impressive ruins. Four-hour weekend workshops include stops at three to four photo-worthy locations in the city—abandoned factories, houses of worship, theaters, and the like. Transportation and photo tips are included. Curious non-photographers are also welcome.

1718 N. Main St., Detroit
517-444-1385 motorcityphotoworkshops.com

KID-FRIENDLY: No
DOG-FRIENDLY: No
HANDICAPPED ACCESSIBLE: No
SEASON: Year-round

HOURS: 7:00 a.m. to noon
COST: $75
EQUIPMENT NEEDED: Camera and gear

34 TOUR DOWNTOWN BY THE QLINE

In a city built around the automobile, Detroit's new downtown streetcar, the QLine, was a big deal when it opened in 2017. Running right through the heart of Detroit, the QLine travels 3.3 miles of Woodward Avenue, from Congress Avenue downtown to Grand Boulevard in New Center. Taken together, the new QLine and its predecessor, the thirty-year-old People Mover, make it possible to visit all of Detroit's downtown attractions on foot and by mass transit—a feat that would have been impossible just a few years ago. The QLine makes twelve stops, passing through the new sports and entertainment center, the District Detroit; bustling Midtown; and the Cultural Center. Key attractions accessed by the QLine include Hart Plaza, Campus Martius, Comerica Park and Ford Field, Little Caesars Arena, the Detroit Symphony Orchestra, the Detroit Institute of Arts, and Wayne State University. Bicycles and strollers are permitted.

qlinedetroit.com

KID-FRIENDLY: Yes

DOG-FRIENDLY: No

HANDICAPPED ACCESSIBLE: Yes

SEASON: Year-round

HOURS: Mon.–Thu. 6:00 a.m. to midnight, Fri. 6:00 a.m. to 2:00 a.m., Sat. 8:00 a.m. to 2:00 a.m., Sun. 8:00 a.m. to 11:00 p.m.

COST: Three-hour pass, $1.50 ($0.75 for seniors and disabled); daily pass, $3; monthly pass, $30; annual pass, $285

EQUIPMENT NEEDED: A little cash and a willingness to chat up the locals. They love it. You will, too.

35 PEDAL AMERICAN-MADE WHEELS AT DETROIT BIKES

Less than half of 1 percent of all the bicycles ridden in the United States were manufactured in this country, and it's time that changed. So goes the thinking at Detroit Bikes, where since 2011 a crew of committed Detroiters has manufactured, assembled, and painted every component of their popular commuter bikes. Detroit Bikes are manufactured in northwest Detroit of American steel and assembled entirely on-site. If you're interested in the process, you can sign up for a factory tour, but if you really want to ride one, head to their Capitol Park storefront. There you can check out a variety of styles, take one for a spin, and buy one. Detroit Bikes are also sold at retailers across the city and around the state. Head to Wheelhouse Detroit if you'd like to rent a bike by the hour and put it through its paces before buying. All Detroit Bikes are sold with a lifetime frame warranty.

Storefront: 1216 Griswold St., Detroit, 313-502-5883
Factory: 13639 Elmira St., Detroit, 313-646-4109
detroitbikes.com

KID-FRIENDLY: Yes

DOG-FRIENDLY: No

HANDICAPPED ACCESSIBLE: Limited

SEASON: Year-round

HOURS: Mon.–Fri. 11:00 a.m. to 7:00 p.m., Sat. 10:00 a.m. to 6:00 p.m.

COST: Bike prices start at $599

EQUIPMENT NEEDED: Your wallet. You'll want to buy a new bike.

36 ADMIRE DETROIT'S MARBLE LIGHTHOUSE

The nation's only art deco lighthouse—and its only marble lighthouse—sits within Michigan's largest city, dedicated to an influential Detroit banker and newspaperman, but it was William Livingstone's role spearheading navigational improvements for ships sailing on the Great Lakes that won him the loudest praise. To honor his achievements, the fifty-eight-foot William Livingstone Memorial Lighthouse was erected on Belle Isle in 1930, designed by superstar art deco architect Albert Kahn. Sculptor Gaza Moroti brought Kahn's creation to life using white Georgia marble, a first for any American lighthouse, a bronze lantern room, and a custom-made three-foot, forty-pound brass light handcrafted in Paris. The lighthouse remains one of the most iconic and photographed landmarks on Belle Isle. Visitors aren't permitted to climb the Livingstone light, but a one-mile walking trail runs around the lighthouse and alongside the adjacent Blue Heron Lagoon, offering great photo opportunities of the unusual lighthouse, the Detroit city skyline, and Windsor.

Belle Isle, 2 Inselruhe Ave., Detroit
313-821-9844 MichiganDNR.com/parksandtrails

KID-FRIENDLY: Yes

DOG-FRIENDLY: Yes

HANDICAPPED ACCESSIBLE: Yes

SEASON: Year-round

HOURS: Monday through Sunday 5:00 a.m. to 10:00 p.m.

COST: Free

EQUIPMENT NEEDED: Good walking shoes. It's a bit of a trek (sometimes a muddy one) from the road out to the lighthouse.

SPECIAL COMMENTS: A recreation passport is required, see page xiv.

37 RUN TO CANADA (AND BACK AGAIN) AT THE DETROIT MARATHON

Not many marathon courses promise the opportunity to run across international borders. The *Detroit Free Press*/Chemical Bank Marathon is one of them. Runners line up at the starting gate near Cobo Center and then run into Canada by way of the Ambassador Bridge at around Mile 3. After a four-mile stretch in Windsor, Ontario, the route veers back into Michigan again, this time through the Detroit-Windsor Tunnel beneath the Detroit River. Other highlights along the 26.2-mile marathon route include the Detroit and Windsor RiverWalks, a circle around Belle Isle, the towers of GM's Renaissance Center, and a dozen live music stages to help keep athletes entertained. The Detroit Marathon takes place annually in mid-October and includes the option of shorter distances: a US-only or international half marathon, a 5K, or a relay race. New for 2018, the Challenge Series offers race combos reminiscent of Detroit's Motown greats: the Temptation (1-mile plus 5K races), the Wonder (one-mile plus 5K and half-marathon races), and the Supreme (one-mile plus 5K and full marathon races). Don't forget your passport!

freepmarathon.com

KID-FRIENDLY: Yes

DOG-FRIENDLY: Yes

HANDICAPPED ACCESSIBLE: Yes

SEASON: October

HOURS: Varies per race

COST: Varies per race; $25–$375

EQUIPMENT NEEDED: Running shoes and your passport

38 HIKE (OR BIKE) THE CLINTON RIVER TRAIL

Many years ago the route followed by the Clinton River Trail was built by Native Americans, a bypass that paralleled the Clinton River and detoured the swamplands between Rochester and Detroit. Then in 1879 the Grand Trunk Railroad took possession of the property, installing a raised railbed along the path. When the railroad abandoned this stretch of line in 1998, the path was quickly redeveloped and opened as a multipurpose rail trail in 2003. The Clinton River Trail stretches sixteen relatively flat miles between Pontiac and Wixom, with surfaces ranging from crushed limestone to pavement. It's ideal for hiking, trail running, as well as mountain and road biking. In spring, a riot of wildflowers and songbirds make the otherwise lightly traveled path especially pleasant. The Clinton River Trail connects two additional metro Detroit multiuse trails, the Bloomfield and the Macomb Orchard trails, making it easy to add additional miles to your outdoor recreation. The Clinton River Trail is part of the larger Great Lake to Lake Trail, which, when complete, will run from Port Huron to South Haven.

clintonrivertrail.org

KID-FRIENDLY: Yes

DOG-FRIENDLY: Yes, on a leash

HANDICAPPED ACCESSIBLE: Varies with surface

SEASON: Year-round

HOURS: Dawn to dusk

COST: Free

EQUIPMENT NEEDED: Good hiking shoes or a bicycle and helmet

39 RENT SOME WHEELS WITH MOGO DETROIT

You'd think the city that put America on four wheels would shun two-wheeled transportation, but Detroit's become a haven for bike riders thanks in part to the success of Slow Roll, launched here in 2010. While many Detroiters cruise the city on their own wheels, the city made it easier for suburban day-trippers and tourists to join in the fun in 2017 with the launch of MoGo, Detroit's first public bike sharing system. MoGo offers 430 bikes at forty-three stations across ten Detroit neighborhoods. Purchase a pass online through Detroit's Transit app or directly at a MoGo station. Then take as many bike trips as you like within your time allotment, returning the bike to the MoGo station of your choice afterward. It's a service designed to offer inexpensive transport without the parking hassle; to provide sustainable, green commuting options; and to allow visitors to see Detroit from a new perspective. Passes are available on a daily, monthly, and annual basis.

mogodetroit.org

KID-FRIENDLY: Yes
DOG-FRIENDLY: No
HANDICAPPED ACCESSIBLE: No
SEASON: Year-round
HOURS: 24 hours a day
COST: Daily pass, $8; monthly pass, $18; annual pass, $80
EQUIPMENT NEEDED: Helmet

40 SPEND HOLIDAY NIGHTS AT GREENFIELD VILLAGE

Henry Ford's personal collection of historic buildings—which range from a Swiss chalet to a collection of Southern slave cottages—once filled his backyard. Today, that section of Henry and Clara Ford's property makes up Greenfield Village, eighty acres' worth of beautifully wooded lawns dotted with noteworthy houses and buildings, historic workshops, and laboratories, but this green expanse may never be lovelier than when it is covered in snow. Leading up to Christmas and New Year's Eve, Holiday Nights at Greenfield Village draw even those who don't like the cold to Dearborn to walk the grounds' lantern-lit paths and tour by horse-drawn sleigh the historic properties decorated for the season. Holiday visitors shop for traditional ornaments, listen to carolers, and snack on roasted nuts. They take a spin on ice skates and meet and greet Santa and his reindeer. When the weather grows too cold, they warm up beside a roaring bonfire. Holiday Nights at Greenfield Village has been named among the most popular yuletide traditions in Michigan.

20900 Oakwood Blvd., Dearborn
313-982-6001 thehenryford.org

KID-FRIENDLY: Yes

DOG-FRIENDLY: No

HANDICAPPED ACCESSIBLE: Yes

SEASON: Mid-April through December

HOURS: 9:30 a.m. to 5:00 p.m.; open daily April 14 to Oct. 28; open Fri.-Sun. Oct. 29 through Nov. 26; occasional evening openings.

COST: $28 for adults, $25.50 for seniors and $21 for youth. If you plan to visit multiple venues at The Henry Ford, save money with a package purchase.

EQUIPMENT NEEDED: Warm clothing and boots, so you can explore the village in the snow.

41 GO PEOPLE WATCHING AT BEACON PARK

Much has been written about downtown Detroit's urban renaissance, but besides renovated high-rises and trendy coffee bars, visitors will find a city made greener by a nice collection of new parks. Beacon Park represents one of Detroit's newest greenspaces, an almost triangular respite bordered by Grand River and Cass Avenues. Unveiled in 2017, the park sits just a few blocks southwest of Grand Circus Park and is frequently busy with impromptu music concerts, food trucks, and drop-in sporting events. Garnering much attention is Lumen, a new, striking, futuristic wood-and-glass restaurant set alongside the park. When the weather is cold, heated sidewalks keep the snow and ice away, while floor-to-ceiling windows allow unimpeded views of Beacon Park. When temperatures rise, the windows open and seating spills out onto the patio, blurring the line between indoors and out. A green roof and LEED-certified status make Lumen a perfect partner for one of Detroit's newest green oases.

1903 Grand River Ave., Detroit
313-566-8250 downtowndetroitparks.com

KID-FRIENDLY: Yes

DOG-FRIENDLY: Yes, on a leash

HANDICAPPED ACCESSIBLE: Yes

SEASON: Year-round

HOURS: 6:00 a.m. to 10:00 p.m.

COST: Free

EQUIPMENT NEEDED: Sunglasses and your wallet, so you can grab a meal at Lumen

42 BICYCLE MIDTOWN, OUTDOORS AND IN

The city that put America on four wheels has become a city greatly enamored of two wheels. The D has become a hot spot for bicycling enthusiasts, thanks in large part to the presence of Slow Roll, Wheelhouse Detroit, the Tour de Troit, and bicycle manufacturers Shinola and Detroit Bikes. Few neighborhoods welcome cyclists more than Midtown, with its pedestrian- and bike-friendly streets and ample bike racks. The neighborhood became even more bicycle friendly in 2017 with the opening of the Lexus Velodrome on the Tolan Playfield, named for Detroiter and track and field Olympian Eddie Tolan. The Velodrome offers world-class bicycle racing on its ten-mile track on most Friday and Saturday nights. Cycling classes, beginning with the basics for age three and up and advancing to skills improvement for all levels are available, and the Lexus Velodrome also offers bicycle riding sessions, running, and walking.

601 Mack Ave., Detroit
313-265-6725 lexusvelodrome.com

KID-FRIENDLY: Yes

DOG-FRIENDLY: No

HANDICAPPED ACCESSIBLE: Yes

SEASON: Year-round

HOURS: Mon.–Fri. 8:00 a.m. to 8:00 p.m., Sat. 7:00 a.m. to 6:00 p.m., Sun. 12:00–4:00 p.m.

COST: Daily passes, $20; Seasonal passes, $200; discounts available for Detroit residents

EQUIPMENT NEEDED: Bicycle and helmet

Photo courtesy of Meadow Brook Hall

FLORA AND FAUNA

43 DIG IN CLARA FORD'S GARDENS AT THE HENRY FORD ESTATE FAIR LANE

With the highly successful Model T and their social status soaring, Henry and Clara Ford constructed a new home in 1915 on thirteen hundred acres of farmland, just a stone's throw from where Greenfield Village sits today. Beyond the estate's opulent mix of English country manor and Midwestern Prairie School styles, beyond its array of buildings—servants' quarters, skating houses, miniature farm buildings, and Henry Ford's private laboratory—Fair Lane became the canvas on which Clara Ford brought to life her hobby: gardening. A sizable greenhouse and acres of elaborate flower beds and rock gardens surround Fair Lane, all of them designed by famed landscape architect Jens Jensen. Except for special functions, Henry Ford's home won't open to the public until an ongoing restoration project is completed, but Fair Lane's grounds are free to explore. Throughout the growing season, dozens of volunteers maintain Clara's vision, cultivating and planting her flower beds, and weeding, pruning, and trimming them throughout the season. Interested volunteers should contact Fair Lane for additional details.

1 Fair Lane Dr., Dearborn
General inquiries: 313-668-3200
Gardening opportunities: 313-668-3195
henryfordfairlane.org

KID-FRIENDLY: Yes

DOG-FRIENDLY: No

HANDICAPPED ACCESSIBLE: Limited

SEASON: Spring through autumn

HOURS: Grounds and gardens 8:00 a.m. to 6:00 p.m.

COST: Free

EQUIPMENT NEEDED: Gardening gear

SPECIAL COMMENTS: Volunteers assist with planting, weeding, mulching, cultivating, pruning, and sweeping on Friday mornings and every other Saturday from April through November.

44 TIPTOE THROUGH THE TULIPS AT THE ANNA SCRIPPS WHITCOMB CONSERVATORY

In 1902 art deco master architect Albert Kahn was commissioned to build an impressive botanical space in the midst of Belle Isle's natural beauty. Originally constructed of a wooden frame, the conservatory's wings and domes were upgraded to steel and aluminum in the 1940s, making the building instantly recognizable on sunny days by its telltale sparkles of metal and glass. In 1955 the conservatory was dedicated to Anna Scripps Whitcomb in thanks for her gift of six hundred brilliantly colored orchids. The conservatory is divided into five distinct sections: an eighty-five-foot Palm House; a Show House with seasonally changing flower displays; a Tropical House with orange, banana, and fig trees; a Cactus House; and a Fernery. Outside, formal gardens complement the lily pond that was added in 1936. The Anna Scripps Whitcomb Conservatory ranks as the oldest continually operating conservatory in the United States. Admission and parking are free with entrance to the island.

2 Inselruhe Ave., Detroit
313-821-9844 belleisleconservancy.org

KID-FRIENDLY: Yes

DOG-FRIENDLY: No

HANDICAPPED ACCESSIBLE: Interior gardens only, though walkways are narrow

SEASON: Year-round

HOURS: Wednesday through Sunday 10:00 a.m. to 5:00 p.m.

COST: Free

EQUIPMENT NEEDED: Camera

SPECIAL COMMENTS: A recreation passport is required, see page xiv.

45 SPY ON BIRDS AT BELLE ISLE

Detroit's location at the convergence of Lake Erie, the Detroit River, Lake St. Clair, and Lake Huron farther north make this southeastern corner of Michigan an ideal spot to watch migratory birds, and Belle Isle's setting in the middle of these waterways renders this state park a great place to see the action. Although the island's natural features were remodeled somewhat by Frederick Law Olmsted and other landscape architects in the 1880s, Belle Isle's abundant green space lures birds with plenty of natural habitat as they fly across the Detroit River on their northern and southern migration routes. The island's ample parking makes it easy for bird lovers to get around with photography gear and scopes. Look for such waterfowl as wood ducks, teals, and terns near Belle Isle's swampland during late fall, winter, and early spring. Woodland birds, such as jays and woodpeckers, can be spied along hiking paths near Lake Okonoka, while songbirds and raptors frequent the park year-round.

2 Inselruhe Ave., Detroit
313-821-9844 belleisleconservancy.org

KID-FRIENDLY: Yes

DOG-FRIENDLY: No

HANDICAPPED ACCESSIBLE: Varies by location

SEASON: Year-round

HOURS: 5:00 a.m. to 10:00 p.m., or after the conclusion of special events

COST: Free

EQUIPMENT NEEDED: Binoculars and a camera

SPECIAL COMMENTS: Recreational passport required, see page xiv

46 CHILL WITH THE PENGUINS AT THE DETROIT ZOO

The world's largest penguinarium, the Polk Penguin Conservation Center, took center stage at the Detroit Zoo when the center opened in 2016. Eighty penguins swim, dive, and waddle in a twenty-five-foot-deep diving tank and past underwater pedestrian tunnels. They're all housed in a building that resembles an iceberg and recalls tales from Ernest Shackleton's legendary 1914 Antarctic expedition aboard the *Endurance*. Although the little birds have received a lot of love since the penguinarium's opening, they aren't the only cold weather creatures with fantastic digs at the 125-acre Detroit Zoo. Other noteworthy exhibits include the Arctic Ring of Life, ranking as one of North America's largest polar bear habitats with its own dive tanks and underwater tunnels, and the Cotton Family Wolf Wilderness Exhibit, which in 2015 debuted the zoo's first wolves since the 1980s. In total the Detroit Zoo houses approximately twenty-five hundred additional animals, from lions, tigers, and bears to a year-round Butterfly Garden.

8450 W. 10 Mile Rd., Royal Oak
248-541-5717 detroitzoo.org

KID-FRIENDLY: Yes

DOG-FRIENDLY: No

HANDICAPPED ACCESSIBLE: Yes

SEASON: Year-round

HOURS: Varies through season

COST: Adults, $18; children (2-18), $15; seniors, $15; military with ID, $15; parking $8. Discounts available for advanced online ticket purchases.

EQUIPMENT NEEDED: Camera and good walking shoes for exploring the rest of the zoo

SPECIAL COMMENTS: The zoo is closed on Thanksgiving day, Christmas day, and New Year's day.

47 RELEASE YOUR INNER SHUTTERBUG AT SUNSET POINT

When Detroit's budget woes were at their worst, many public greenspaces were left untended. Perhaps chief among them was Belle Isle, long a beloved Detroit landmark, abandoned while the city waited for better days and a beefier checkbook. In 2009 the Belle Isle Women's Committee introduced their first efforts at bringing the popular island back with a newly designed corner christened Sunset Point. As the name implies, the triangle-shaped western corner of Belle Isle is best experienced at dusk. When the sun slides beneath the horizon, it casts a rainbow-sherbet glow over the Ambassador Bridge, the Detroit RiverWalk, the towers of the GM Renaissance Center, and the rest of Detroit's skyline. In the foreground, the sparkling Detroit River, the massive white Scott Memorial Fountain, and thirteen acres of flower gardens add photographic appeal. Since its transformation to a Michigan state park in 2014, Belle Isle charges a nominal admission fee.

2 Inselruhe Ave., Detroit
313-821-9844 belleisleconservancy.org

KID-FRIENDLY: Yes
DOG-FRIENDLY: Yes
HANDICAPPED ACCESSIBLE: Yes
SEASON: Year-round
HOURS: 6:00 a.m. to 11:00 p.m.

COST: Free
EQUIPMENT NEEDED: Camera
SPECIAL COMMENTS: Recreational passport required if driving into the park, see page xiv.

48 ENJOY THE WILDFLOWERS AT WILLIAM G. MILLIKEN STATE PARK

Not too many years ago this thirty-one-acre stretch of downtown Detroit's RiverWalk was an embarrassing expanse of decaying parking lots and a dilapidated harbor wall. The decade-long redevelopment of this stretch of Detroit not only transformed the area into one of America's loveliest waterways but also resulted in a brand-new state park, Michigan's first in an urban setting. Besides being connected seamlessly to the wildly popular Detroit RiverWalk, William G. Milliken State Park offers a fifty-two-slip harbor with transient boat rental space; a fishing pier; a photogenic white lighthouse; native wetlands; sightings of native songbirds, pheasants, muskrats, and foxes; picnic and grilling facilities; and numerous plantings of ornamental and natural wildflowers. Interpretive signs explain the unique natural habit here on the Detroit River. Although Michigan typically requires a recreation passport to visit its state parks, Milliken State Park's integration with the Detroit RiverWalk makes this a rare example of an admission-free state park.

1900 Atwater St., Detroit
313-396-0217 michigandnr.com/parksandtrails

KID-FRIENDLY: Yes

DOG-FRIENDLY: Yes, on a leash

HANDICAPPED ACCESSIBLE: Yes

SEASON: Year-round

HOURS: 6:00 a.m. to 10:00 p.m.

COST: Free

EQUIPMENT NEEDED: Camera and comfortable walking shoes

49 FEED THE DEER AT BELLE ISLE NATURE CENTER

No one's quite sure how a herd of European fallow deer made their way to Detroit in the late nineteenth century, but legend has it that in 1895 the president of France, Felix Faure, gave the deer to the city with the intent that they would populate a deer park on Belle Isle. However these deer arrived, their presence has long been associated with the island. Today's herd is directly related to those original deer and vary in color from white to dark brown. Since they turned out to be reasonably docile creatures, modern-day visitors to Belle Isle Nature Center's deer encounter are permitted to pet and feed the creatures. Other animals on display at the Nature Center are true Michigan natives: toads and frogs, half a dozen turtle varieties, rat snakes, and several freshwater fish. The Belle Isle Nature Center is affiliated with the Detroit Zoo. Admission is free with entrance to the island.

176 Lakeside Dr., Detroit
313-852-4056 belleislenaturecenter.detroitzoo.org

KID-FRIENDLY: Yes
DOG-FRIENDLY: No
HANDICAPPED ACCESSIBLE: Yes
SEASON: Year-round
HOURS: 10:00 a.m to 5:00 p.m.
COST: Free

EQUIPMENT NEEDED: Camera and some cash to feed the deer
SPECIAL COMMENTS: Recreational passport required if driving into the park, see page xiv.

50 STROLL THROUGH THE FLOWER BEDS AT GABRIEL RICHARD PARK

Just a few short years ago Gabriel Richard Park was little more than a dismal, forgotten stretch of the Detroit River, but in 2015 this park found new life thanks to the preservation efforts of the Detroit River Conservancy and the transformative Detroit RiverWalk project. Located alongside the graceful white arches of the MacArthur Bridge to Belle Isle, Gabriel Richard Park positively bursts with color in warm weather months when vivid flower gardens simply spill out of their spacious beds. The green oasis also includes a colorful butterfly garden and viewing scopes for spying on the wildlife and birds that frequent the park (interpretive signs help identify the birds and tell visitors what else to look for). Also on-site are fishing stations, a meditative labyrinth, an amusing fountain, and restrooms. A pavilion and park benches make it easy to linger in this lovely revitalized span of the Detroit River.

E. Jefferson Ave. at E. Grand Blvd., Detroit
detroitriverfront.org

KID-FRIENDLY: Yes

DOG-FRIENDLY: Yes, on a leash

HANDICAPPED ACCESSIBLE: Yes

SEASON: Year-round

HOURS: 6:00 a.m. to 10:00 p.m.

COST: Free

EQUIPMENT NEEDED: Camera and good walking shoes

51 BECOME A CITIZEN FORESTER WITH THE GREENING OF DETROIT

Much has been made in recent years about the downsizing of Detroit. As urban residents moved out—either to the suburbs or farther afield—whole city blocks were left abandoned. Houses fell into disrepair. Fallow lots became choked with litter and weeds. The mission of the Greening of Detroit is to reclaim those blighted places by planting trees, building greenspaces, and offering environmental education and job training to residents in the process. Each year three thousand to five thousand volunteers become citizen foresters, training and leading landscaping teams, planting trees and urban gardens, and cleaning up parks. Training sessions instruct volunteers in how to successfully plant and maintain small trees and gardens. Then they head out across the city to foster the Greening of Detroit. Community-grown fruits, vegetables, and flowers are harvested by volunteers, too, for delivery to community food banks, church pantries, and the volunteers who worked the soil. Visit the organization's website to learn about upcoming training sessions and opportunities to plant, prune, and maintain trees and vegetable gardens across Detroit.

13000 West McNichols Rd., Detroit
313-237-8733 greeningofdetroit.com

CHILD FRIENDLY: Yes

DOG FRIENDLY: No

HANDICAPPED ACCESSIBLE: No

SEASON: Spring through Autumn

HOURS: Varies per event

COST: Free

EQUIPMENT NEEDED: Good walking shoes and gardening gloves

52 EXPERIENCE FLOWER DAY AT EASTERN MARKET

Since 1967 Detroit's most famous market—and its oldest—has celebrated the arrival of spring with Flower Day. Held annually the Sunday after Mother's Day, the market offers a wide range of flowers, from hardy, cold-weather violets and pansies to warm weather-loving lilies, daisies, and coneflowers. All the flowers on display were transported from throughout southeast Michigan and southern Ontario with an eye toward the Great Lakes State's growing season. In total you'll find fifteen acres of flowers hardy enough for planting in springtime Michigan and vendors willing to provide planting advice along with their flowers. Since 1841 Detroiters have purchased their flowers, meat, and produce at Eastern Market, making this one of the oldest farmers markets in the United States. Plan to while away a whole morning strolling through Eastern Market's six sheds that spread across four and a half acres and several city blocks near the heart of downtown.

2934 Russell St., Detroit
easternmarket.com

KID-FRIENDLY: Yes

DOG-FRIENDLY: No

HANDICAPPED ACCESSIBLE: Yes

SEASON: Year-round

HOURS: 7:00 a.m. to 5:00 p.m.

COST: Free

EQUIPMENT NEEDED: Camera, wallet and a shopping basket

53 LEARN ABOUT TREES AND HISTORY AT ELMWOOD CEMETERY

In 2015 Detroit was awarded its first certified arboretum, and the greenspace happens to be one of the city's most important cemeteries. Since 1846 Elmwood has served as the final resting place for Detroit's dearly departed: prominent industrialists and abolitionists; once-famous politicians and honored veterans. Audio tours help visitors find their way among the who's who buried here, but the historic cemetery's reputation as a first-rate arboretum can be traced to famed landscape architect Frederick Law Olmsted, whose redesign of Elmwood in 1890 added towering hardwoods and flowering trees to complement the landscape's gentle stream and rolling hills. Olmsted's artistry accentuated the natural contours of these eighty-six acres and heightened the impact of Elmwood's stately memorial markers. Visitors can find their way through more than eighty species of trees using self-guided tour maps. Or they can join one of many guided tree tours, identifying trees, spotting numerous bird species, and learning about the cemetery's history through such organizations as the Detroit Audubon Society, Wild Birds Unlimited, Greening of Detroit, and the Detroit Garden Center.

1200 Elmwood Ave., Detroit
313-567-3453 elmwoodhistoriccemetery.org

KID-FRIENDLY: Yes, age 5 and up

DOG-FRIENDLY: No

HANDICAPPED ACCESSIBLE: No

SEASON: Guided tours May through September

HOURS: May through September, 7:00 a.m. to 7:00 p.m. daily; October through April, 8:30 a.m. to 4:00 p.m. daily.

COST: Free

EQUIPMENT NEEDED: Camera and good walking shoes

COMERICA PARK (page 144)

MOTOR CITY BREW TOURS (page 134)

AQUARIUM
OPEN

BELLE ISLE AQUARIUM & CONSERVATORY (pages 102)

DETROIT SKYLINE FROM RIVERWALK (page 35)

DETROIT CITY FOOTBALL CLUB (page 156)

YOU ONLY
BROUGHT
YOUR

GREENFIELD VILLAGE (page 36)

DETROIT ZOO PENGUINARIUM (page 69)

DETROIT BIKES (page 51)

ONE WAY

MURALS IN EASTERN MARKET (page 110)

MILLIKEN STATE PARK (page 71)

VINTAGE BASE BALL AT GREENFIELD VILLAGE (page 142)

DETROIT BOAT CLUB CREW (page 2)

***PYLON* BY ISAMU NOGUCHI, HART PLAZA** (page 138)

54 STROLL THE GROUNDS OF THE EDSEL AND ELEANOR FORD HOUSE

Henry Ford's only son, Edsel, and his wife, Eleanor, weren't hurting for money when in 1926 they commissioned noted architect Albert Kahn to design their family home on Lake St. Clair. The Fords were going after a Cotswold cottage effect with this elegant brick estate. Inside, the thirty-thousand-square-foot house looks just as it did when the Fords lived here, complete with sixteenth-century wood paneling and stone fireplaces salvaged from post-war Europe, but the estate's grounds are nearly as remarkable. Celebrated landscape architect Jens Jensen molded the eighty-six-acre grounds to his vision in the 1920s. The gardens' play of shadow and light and their engagement of all the senses are hallmarks of a Jensen project, and while the estate's meadows, water features, and rock formations look perfectly natural, all were meticulously designed and crafted by the master gardener. Guided bird walks as well as grounds and garden tours explore the property's highlights and expand on Jensen's story. A new visitor center currently under construction is slated to open in early 2020.

1100 Lake Shore Rd., Grosse Pointe Shores
313-884-4222 fordhouse.org

KID-FRIENDLY: Yes

DOG-FRIENDLY: No

HANDICAPPED ACCESSIBLE: Limited

SEASON: Spring through autumn

HOURS: Tues.–Sat. 9:00 a.m. to 6:00 p.m., Sun. 11:00 a.m. to 6:00 p.m.

COST: Adults, $12; seniors, $11; children, $8

EQUIPMENT NEEDED: Camera and good walking shoes

55 ENJOY FALL FOLIAGE ALONG THE PAINT CREEK TRAIL

Michigan's first nonmotorized rail-to-trail park opened to the public in 1983. Extending northwest out of Rochester to Lake Orion, the 8.9-mile linear park began as a rail bed for the Michigan Central Railroad Company in 1872. Over the years, passengers and freight made their way throughout Michigan and beyond until train service was halted in the 1970s. In 1981 the route found new life as the Paint Creek Trail, a multiuse, crushed limestone path popular with bicyclists, hikers, and horseback riders. While the Paint Creek Trail is particularly attractive in the warmth of summer and cross-country skiers and snowshoers frequent the path in winter, the trail is remarkably beautiful in autumn. Maple and birch trees form a canopy over the trail, taking on brilliant shades of red and yellow. Another reason to visit in the fall? The town of Goodison, at the trail's halfway point, is home to two cider mills, both within close proximity to the Paint Creek Trail.

Rochester
248-651-9260 paintcreektrail.org

KID-FRIENDLY: Yes

DOG-FRIENDLY: Yes, on a leash

HANDICAPPED ACCESSIBLE: Yes

SEASON: Year-round

HOURS: Half-hour before sunrise to half-hour after sunset

COST: Free

EQUIPMENT NEEDED: Camera and good walking shoes

56 SEE MEADOW BROOK IN BLOOM

Considered one of the finest examples of Tudor-revival architecture in America, the palatial Meadow Brook Hall was constructed in 1926 by Matilda Dodge Wilson, widow of automobile manufacturing magnate John Dodge, and her second husband, lumberman Alfred Wilson. Historic tours of Meadow Brook are immensely popular. The eighty-eight-thousand-square-foot mansion wows visitors with its leaded glass windows and opulent wood paneling, its art deco tile work, and oversized stone fireplaces, but the grounds are no less impressive. Visitors get an overview of Meadow Brook's grounds on standard Walking Estate tours, but the real treat for lovers of the outdoors comes in summer when the weeklong Meadow Brook in Bloom festival celebrates all things floral. Self-guided tours lead through sixteen gardens. Fresh flowers adorn each of the hall's rooms. Fashion and photo displays provide fresh insight into the Dodge family, and docents reveal rare glimpses of the original flower room, where the head groundskeeper once arranged bouquets of flowers to brighten Matilda's rooms.

350 Estate Dr., Rochester Hills
248-364-6200 meadowbrookhall.org

KID-FRIENDLY: Yes

DOG-FRIENDLY: No

HANDICAPPED ACCESSIBLE: The Hall, yes; grounds, limited

SEASON: The Hall, year-round; grounds, spring through autumn

HOURS: 10:45 a.m. to 4:00 p.m.; daily tours start at 11:00 a.m.

COST: Group tour, $10 for adults and $5 for children

EQUIPMENT NEEDED: Camera

57 EXPLORE THE NATION'S OLDEST AQUARIUM AT BELLE ISLE

The Belle Isle Aquarium opened to the public in 1904, a Beaux-Arts gem designed by architectural virtuoso Albert Kahn that ranks as the oldest aquarium in the United States. At its opening, Belle Isle Aquarium was the third largest in the world. Saltwater was shipped in from the ocean to fill the aquarium's tanks, each intended to look like a work of art hanging on vaulted walls. The walls were in turn covered with rare green opalite glass tiles that create a shimmering underwater effect. In spite of the aquarium's historical and design significance, the Belle Isle Aquarium was shuttered for some years beginning in 2005. Detroit's revitalization and the island's transformation into a state park freed up funds to refurbish the building, a project that continues to this day. Animals on display range from native fish, such as white and yellow perch and pumpkinseed sunfish, to more exotic creatures, such as seahorses, koi, and clownfish. Admission and parking are free with entrance to Belle Isle State Park.

900 Inselruhe Ave., Detroit
313-402-0466 detroitaquarium.weebly.com

KID-FRIENDLY: Yes

DOG-FRIENDLY: No

HANDICAPPED ACCESSIBLE: Yes

SEASON: Year-round

HOURS: Friday through Sunday 10:00 a.m. to 4:00 p.m.

COST: Free admission and free parking

EQUIPMENT NEEDED: Camera and patience—the aquarium is popular with school groups

SPECIAL COMMENTS: Recreational passport required if driving into the park, see page xiv.

58 ZIP THROUGH THE TREES AT TREERUNNER ADVENTURE PARK

Ten aerial trails and a zip line weave through the thick treetops at West Bloomfield's TreeRunner Adventure Park northwest of Detroit. Michigan's largest forest climbing park, TreeRunner Adventure Park is outfitted with a series of wooden platforms constructed atop the park's hardwood trees. The platforms are in turn connected by a series of rope walkways and floating bridges that snake here and there through the treetops. Visitors make their way through 140 aerial challenges chosen from among five varying difficulty levels, each of them color coded, to chart their way through TreeRunner's circuitous course. Depending upon difficulty levels and the trails selected, most climbers are able to make their way along three or four trails over the course of their three-hour adventure session. Visitors who attend late in the day, during Twilight Hours, enjoy price savings and the thrill of climbing the trees illuminated with tiny white lights. Reservations are required.

6600 W. Maple Rd., West Bloomfield Twp.
248-242-7022, treerunnerwestbloomfield.com

KID-FRIENDLY: Yes, age 5 and up

DOG-FRIENDLY: No

HANDICAPPED ACCESSIBLE: No

SEASON: May through September

HOURS: Summer: 9:00 a.m. to 8 p.m. (open until 10:00 p.m. Fri.–Sat.); fall: Fri. 3:00–10:00 p.m., Sat. 9:00 a.m. to 10:00 p.m., Sun. 9:00 a.m. to 8:00 p.m.

COST: Adults 12 and older, $48; children 10-11, $43; children 7-9, $38; children 5-6, $1 (each child must be accompanied by an adult)

EQUIPMENT NEEDED: Camera and good walking shoes

59 TAP A MAPLE TREE AT ONE OF DETROIT'S METROPARKS

It's one of the finest rewards for enduring Michigan's long, brutal winters: the sweet pleasure of maple syrup. When the worst of Mother Nature's frigid temperatures pass, southeast Michigan's maple trees slowly come to life, sending sap upward to restore the leaves—and provide hungry humans with a little something sweet. In Metroparks across Macomb, Oakland, Washtenaw, and Wayne counties, naturalists guide visitors through the process of maple sap collection, explaining the science behind the process and sharing the importance of maple syrup and tree tapping to Native American and Anglo communities in early America. Naturalists demonstrate how to select the best trees in your own yard and then help visitors tap Metropark trees and boil the sap down into syrup and sugar. Some Metroparks also offer craft making and the opportunity to taste-test maple syrup and sugar. Tapping maple trees typically occurs in late February or March but depends on the weather. Call ahead to verify dates.

Indian Springs Metropark
5200 Indian Trail, White Lake
248-625-7280, metroparks.com

Kensington Metropark
4570 Huron River Pkwy., Milford
248-684-8632, metroparks.com

Oakwoods Metropark
32911 Willow Rd., New Boston
734-782-3956, metroparks.com

Wolcott Mill Metropark Farm Center
65775 Wolcott Rd., Ray
586-752-5932, metroparks.com

KID-FRIENDLY: Yes

DOG-FRIENDLY: No

HANDICAPPED ACCESSIBLE: Varies by park

SEASON: Late winter/early spring

HOURS: Varies by park

COST: Varies by park

EQUIPMENT NEEDED: Warm clothing—spring can be cold in Detroit

60 TAKE A BIRD-THEMED FIELD TRIP WITH THE DETROIT AUDUBON SOCIETY

An abundance of fresh water surrounds Detroit: Lake Erie, the Detroit River, Lake St. Clair, and Lake Huron, and two migratory bird routes, the Atlantic and Mississippi Flyways, overlap in southeastern Michigan, making this an ideal spot for birdwatchers. Detroit and Windsor-area islands Grosse Ile, Belle Isle, Peche Island, Fighting Island, and a dozen others serve as stepping stones across the Great Lakes waterways for birds making their way north and south. The Detroit Audubon Society helps locals spot and identify native and migratory birds through monthly nature programs, weekend birdwatching outings, and bird-themed field trips. In 2018 trips ranged from owl prowls to "frog symphonies," where attendees learn to identify frogs by sound; from pheasant walks to wildlife explorations of Detroit's Magee Marsh, the latter considered one of the finest spots in North America to see migrating warblers and songbirds. Visit the Detroit Audubon's website for a list of current events.

detroitaudubon.org

KID-FRIENDLY: Yes

DOG-FRIENDLY: No

HANDICAPPED ACCESSIBLE: Varies by program

SEASON: Year-round

HOURS: Dawn until dusk

COST: Varies by event, free to $20

EQUIPMENT NEEDED: Binoculars and a camera

SPECIAL COMMENTS: Events taking place on Belle Isle require a Michigan recreation passport

Photo courtesy of Amy S. Eckert

FOOD AND CULTURE

61 WATCH ARTISTS AT WORK AT MURALS IN THE MARKET

Nearly fifty artists from around the world descend upon Detroit each September, paints and brushes in hand, to cover a new stretch of Eastern Market's city walls with art. Since 2013, Detroit-based art firm 1XRUN and its gallery Inner State have curated more than one hundred murals in Eastern Market alone, and more than two hundred citywide. The murals range from brightly colored to dull, from cartoonish to photographic, from whimsical to fantastic and even political. Visitors can watch mural artists in action, creating the year's newest batch of artworks, at Murals in the Market. The ten-day art-themed street party allows opportunities to engage with and ask questions of the artists, to attend panel discussions and artist dinners, and to enjoy live music and entertainment. When the festival wraps up, tour Eastern Market's murals by way of their online map, a printed map available at Eastern Market businesses, or join one of several guided trips through the murals, such as those offered by Motor City Brew Tours, Wheelhouse Detroit, the Detroit Experience Factory, and Detroit Segway.

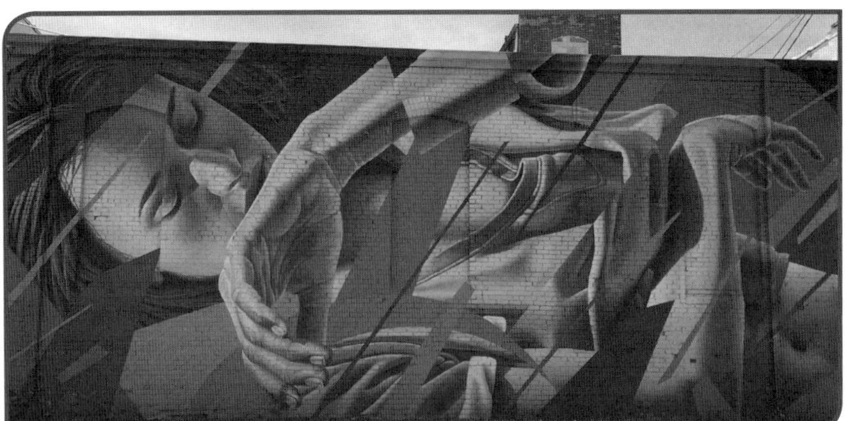

muralsinthemarket.com

KID-FRIENDLY: Yes

DOG-FRIENDLY: Yes, on a leash

HANDICAPPED ACCESSIBLE: Yes

SEASON: Festival annually in September, murals year-round

HOURS: Daily

COST: Viewing murals is always free, but there may be charges for certain festival events

EQUIPMENT NEEDED: Good walking shoes and a camera

62 CELEBRATE THE SEASON AT NOEL NIGHT

Each year more than a hundred cultural institutions, galleries, and boutiques throw open their doors for one glorious winter open house in Detroit's Midtown neighborhood. Noel Night brings all of Detroit together in a celebration of the approaching holiday season. Admission is free at such museums as the Detroit Institute of Arts, the Michigan Science Center, the Charles H. Wright Museum of African American History, and the Detroit Historical Museum, but also on tap are free music performances, drinks, and snack stations tucked within museum gallery spaces. At boutiques and art galleries around Midtown, you'll find discounted shopping, free holiday craft stations for adults and children, live music, food, and drink. Mr. and Mrs. Claus put in several appearances on Noel Night, too, and horse-drawn carriages transport holiday revelers through Detroit's snowy city streets in style. Noel Night persistently ranks as one of Midtown Detroit's most anticipated yuletide events. You can find a detailed schedule and Noel Night map online.

noelnight.org

KID-FRIENDLY: Yes

DOG-FRIENDLY: Yes, outside and on a leash

HANDICAPPED ACCESSIBLE: Varies with venue

SEASON: December

HOURS: Holiday activities take place the evening of the first Saturday in December.

COST: Free

EQUIPMENT NEEDED: Warm clothing, good walking shoes and your wallet

63 TOUR DETROIT'S GALLERIES ON SECOND SATURDAYS

Named a UNESCO Design City in 2015—and still today the only American city designated as such by UNESCO—Detroit has long enjoyed a reputation for superb creativity. See for yourself the extent of the artistic talent at galleries and art museums across the city. Fifty independent galleries open their doors late on Second Saturdays each month to encourage Detroiters on an evening cultural stroll. Featured galleries lie across the city and include the Library Street Collective and the Carr Center downtown, Playground Detroit and the Wasserman Projects in Eastern Market, and the Detroit Artists Market and MOCAD in Midtown. A complete listing of participating galleries can be seen online divided by city and neighborhood to make planning easy. The website also offers a comprehensive listing of Detroit's major art galleries and museums, including those who choose not to participate in Second Saturdays, so you can build your own art-themed tour of The D.

artdetroitnow.com

KID-FRIENDLY: Yes
DOG-FRIENDLY: No
HANDICAPPED ACCESSIBLE: Yes
SEASON: Year-round
HOURS: 12:00–6:00 p.m.
COST: See website
EQUIPMENT NEEDED: Good walking shoes

64 DISCOVER THE WORLD OF JAZZ AT THE DETROIT JAZZ FESTIVAL

Each Labor Day weekend Hart Plaza and Campus Martius in downtown Detroit come alive with the sounds of the world's largest free jazz festival. Launched in 1980, the festival was part of an effort to lure people downtown with the sounds of world-class jazz. In those early days, the Detroit Jazz Festival partnered with the highly touted international jazz festival in Montreux, Switzerland, sharing designs for promotional posters and merchandise, and even swapping performers from one side of the Atlantic to the other. The modern Detroit Jazz Festival stands alone, with more than one hundred artists performing in concert on five stages spread along Woodward Avenue. Attendees can wander from Hart Plaza on the Detroit River northward to Campus Martius to catch various acts. Besides live music performances, the festival includes food tents, music workshops for adults and children, jam sessions, and the chance to meet and greet some of jazz's most accomplished musicians.

detroitjazzfest.com

KID-FRIENDLY: Yes
DOG-FRIENDLY: No
HANDICAPPED ACCESSIBLE: Limited
SEASON: Labor Day weekend
HOURS: One weekend only
COST: Free; VIP tickets available
EQUIPMENT NEEDED: Comfortable shoes and patience—the crowds can be large

65 PEDAL FOR YOUR DRINKS WITH THE HANDLEBAR

Detroit's pedal-powered pub launched in downtown Detroit in 2015. Like its counterpart, the Detroit Cycle Boat, the HandleBar combines exercise, a sight-seeing tour of downtown Detroit, and a bar. The party pub departs from near Campus Martius Park loaded with drinks, snacks, a nice sound system, and a designated driver (a "Bar Handler"). Then guests pedal out into the streets of downtown Detroit for a tour of the city's shops, Greektown, Little Caesars Arena, and Comerica Park, stopping at bars and restaurants along the route. The Bar Handler leads the way, but tours are customizable. Since only ten of the HandleBar's sixteen seats have pedals, there's opportunity to take a break if you want to. A flat rate buys exclusive use of the HandleBar for two hours. The bar has space to accommodate as few as six and as many as sixteen passengers. All riders must be at least eighteen years old.

190 Gratiot Ave., Detroit
handlebardetroit.com

KID-FRIENDLY: No

DOG-FRIENDLY: No

HANDICAPPED ACCESSIBLE: No

SEASON: Year-round

HOURS: Monday through Friday 12:30–10:00 p.m., Saturday and Sunday 10:00 a.m. to 10:00 p.m.

COST: Individual seat $25 to $400 for a group

EQUIPMENT NEEDED: Sunblock

66 SEE DETROIT'S CITYSCAPE WITH DETROIT URBAN ADVENTURES

Greektown was, as its name suggests, the historic neighborhood of Detroit's Greek residents in the early 1900s. The city's immigrants left their mark on this neighborhood with Mediterranean restaurants, bakeries, and markets that remain popular today. The art deco Guardian Building, constructed in 1929, has wowed passers-by for nearly a century with an exterior covered in nearly two million tangerine-colored bricks, and the Wurlitzer Building, once the world's largest music house with fourteen stories of concert space, a music store, and a recording studio, was transformed into the stylish Siren Hotel in 2018. Detroit's culture and history, from the city's heyday to its much-publicized economic bust and recent resurgence, take center stage on briskly paced, two-hour walking tours led by Detroit Urban Adventures. Conducted by a native Detroiter, the urban tours follow several themes, ranging from the city's current highlights to its ethnic neighborhoods and its modern-day rebirth as one of America's most interesting urban centers. Tours include coney dog nibbles and a sampling of locally brewed beer.

313-701-1900 detroiturbanadventures.com

KID-FRIENDLY: Yes

DOG-FRIENDLY: Yes, on a leash

HANDICAPPED ACCESSIBLE: Varies with tour

SEASON: Year-round

HOURS: 8:00 a.m. to 8:00 p.m.

COST: Tours $27

EQUIPMENT NEEDED: Good walking shoes and a camera

67 WITNESS THE COMEBACK CITY WITH THE DETROIT EXPERIENCE FACTORY

You'll be hard pressed to find a tour experience more inspiring than what you find at the Detroit Experience Factory, and it will be difficult to find travel guides more spirited and enthusiastic about their city than those at DXF. The richness—and occasionally the absurdities—of Detroit history, the depth of the city's cultural experiences, the tales of movers, shakers, and ordinary folk make their way into the guided tours offered by the DXF. Themes range from walking tours of Corktown to African American-owned bars; from Midtown's Cultural Center to Detroit's finest coffee, tea, and chocolate. Tours take place on foot, by People Mover or Qline, and occasionally by bus, depending upon the destination and theme. You can also pop into the DXF's Visitor Center on Monroe Street for a quick bit of free advice: Where should I have dinner tonight? Where can we enjoy a romantic nightcap? What's going on this weekend in Detroit's theaters, ball parks, and concert venues?

440 Burroughs St., Detroit
313-962-4590 detroitexperiencefactory.org

KID-FRIENDLY: Varies with tour

DOG-FRIENDLY: Varies with tour

HANDICAPPED ACCESSIBLE: Varies with tour

SEASON: Year-round

HOURS: Monday through Friday 10:00 a.m. to 5:00 p.m., Saturday 10:30 a.m. to 4:30 p.m.

COST: Prices vary from free to $15

EQUIPMENT NEEDED: Good walking shoes and a camera

68 EXPLORE THE OUTDOOR SCULPTURES AT CRANBROOK ACADEMY OF ART

One of the nation's preeminent art and science institutions, Cranbrook embodied the best of the arts and crafts movement at the turn of the twentieth century, joining together architectural and creative geniuses Eliel and Eero Saarinen, Albert Kahn, Carl Milles, Marshall Fredericks, and Charles and Ray Eames to teach, study, and design in metro Detroit. Cranbrook's vast grounds are adorned with sculptures, many of them by these artistic dons. Take an art-themed walk to see a fifth-century Chinese lion statue; several Carl Milles bronzes; wrought iron gates designed by Eliel Saarinen; and a number of granite sculptures by Marshall Fredericks, famous for Detroit's beloved *Spirit of Detroit* statue at the Coleman A. Young Municipal Center downtown. Cranbrook's fourteen-page Outdoor Sculpture Guide provides a detailed self-guided walking tour online. If you have time, visit Cranbrook's art museum, with works ranging from those by Cranbrook's founders to those produced by the institute's current student body; the art deco Saarinen house, built by Eliel himself; and the Smith House, designed by Frank Lloyd Wright.

39221 Woodward Ave., Bloomfield Hills
248-645-3300 cranbrookart.edu

KID-FRIENDLY: Yes

DOG-FRIENDLY: Yes, on a leash

HANDICAPPED ACCESSIBLE: Limited

SEASON: Grounds and Art Museum, year-round; historic houses, May through October

HOURS: Monday through Friday 9:00 a.m. to 5:00 p.m.

COST: Free

EQUIPMENT NEEDED: Camera, good walking shoes, and a downloadable tour guide

69 FEEL THE ENERGY AT MOVEMENT ELECTRONIC MUSIC FESTIVAL

For one glorious weekend in May, all of downtown Detroit pulses with the music of Movement, an internationally recognized electronic music extravaganza. More than one hundred artists—local celebs as well as innovators in the field of electronic and techno music—perform on five stages in downtown's Hart Plaza, set right on the banks of the Detroit River. The centerpiece of the festival is, naturally, Movement's live performances, but the event also incorporates visual art projects. You'll also see vendors selling music and audio technology, too, making the festival something of a resource for those who wish to create their own music. Launched as the Detroit Electronic Music Festival back in 2000—and still referred to as DEMF by longtime festivalgoers—Movement takes place in the heart of the city that invented techno decades ago. A one-day or full weekend wristband makes it possible to come and go to a variety of events.

Hart Plaza, Detroit
movement.us

KID-FRIENDLY: Varies with concert

DOG-FRIENDLY: Yes, on a leash

HANDICAPPED ACCESSIBLE: Yes

SEASON: Memorial Day weekend

HOURS: Varies

COST: Day pass, $85; three-day pass, $195

EQUIPMENT NEEDED: Comfortable shoes and patience (the crowds can be large)

70 DISCOVER PUBLIC ART IN THE PEOPLE MOVER

Even though Detroit unveiled its new QLine system in 2017, the elevated monorail system called the People Mover remains a good means of getting around. The People Mover's three-mile loop incorporates destinations inaccessible by the QLine, the Cobo Center, the Renaissance Center, and Greektown among them, and the train's elevated track offers a bird's-eye view of downtown. While you're exploring the city on foot and by public transport, take note of the art within each of the People Mover's thirteen stations. Fifteen artists (nine of them from Michigan) created these site-specific works, many of them constructed of Detroit-made Pewabic tiles. Favorites include *The Blue Nile*, a rendition of an African Noah's Ark by Charles McGee at the Broadway station; *Catching Up*, the realistic statue of a man reading a newspaper by J. Seward Johnson Jr. at Grand Circus Park; and *Cavalcade of Cars*, a large mural of seven vintage automobiles by Larry Ebel and Linda Cianciolo Scarlett at the Cobo Center stop.

thepeoplemover.com

KID-FRIENDLY: Yes

DOG-FRIENDLY: No

HANDICAPPED ACCESSIBLE: Yes

SEASON: Year-round

HOURS: Monday through Friday 9:00 a.m. to 5:00 p.m., with extended hours during summer and special events

COST: $0.75 per ride; monthly passes, $10; annual pass, $100

EQUIPMENT NEEDED: Cash or People Mover tokens, available in the stations

71 CYCLE URBAN GARDENS WITH WHEELHOUSE DETROIT

Detroit's urban gardens have gotten a lot of attention in recent years. It's not uncommon to see locally grown produce on market shelves and restaurant menus. The produce has often been raised on one of the fifteen hundred urban gardens sprinkled across the city on property that was once occupied by Detroit's abandoned houses. Bicycle vendor Wheelhouse Detroit guides visitors to some of the city's most interesting gardens, leading guests on two wheels past tidy vegetable plots and spacious greenhouses. Guides share insight as to why Detroit grew into such a sprawling city; how The D came to have so many empty buildings; and the innovative programs that popped up to reclaim idle land, teach Detroiters how to garden, and funnel the results into a unique food culture. Wheelhouse Detroit offers a variety of themed bicycle tours, including highlights of Corktown, Haunted Detroit, Cigars in Detroit, Sports Heritage, and Techno in the 313. Not into group tours? Rent a bike and pedal solo along the sparkling Detroit RiverWalk or the paved rail trail, the Dequindre Cut.

Rivard Plaza on the Detroit RiverWalk
1340 E. Atwater St., Detroit
313-656-2453 wheelhousedetroit.com

KID-FRIENDLY: Yes

DOG-FRIENDLY: No

HANDICAPPED ACCESSIBLE: No

SEASON: Year-round

HOURS: Monday through Saturday 10:00 a.m. to 8:00 p.m., Sunday 10:00 a.m. to 5:00 p.m.

COST: Adult rentals start at $15 for two hours

EQUIPMENT NEEDED: Sunglasses, sunblock and a camera

72 CHECK OUT THE RIDES AT THE WOODWARD DREAM CRUISE

The sounds of souped-up V-8s signal the arrival of Camaros, Mustangs, and an array of Detroit's muscle cars. Meticulously restored Chevy Bel Airs draw oohs and aahs, their fins painted turquoise or candy pink. Boxy Ford Model A's remind spectators of the Motor City's roots, and there's enough chrome in sight to make sunglasses essential. These are the sights and sounds of the Woodward Dream Cruise. Originally launched to raise funds for a children's soccer field, the cruise has since exploded into the largest one-day automotive event in the world. Each year the Woodward Dream Cruise attracts 1.5 million visitors from across the globe to a sixteen-mile parade of more than forty thousand restored cars, most of them built in Detroit's automotive heydays of the 1950s and '60s. Smokin'-hot Corvettes, Trans Ams, and other muscle cars share the road with beautifully restored Edsels, Studebakers, and Corvairs on a cruise down America's first highway, Highway 1, an extension of Detroit's Woodward Avenue. The Dream Cruise lasts about twelve hours, and attendance is free.

Woodward Ave. between Ferndale and Pontiac
woodwarddreamcruise.com

KID-FRIENDLY: Yes

DOG-FRIENDLY: Yes, on a leash

HANDICAPPED ACCESSIBLE: Yes

SEASON: August

HOURS: All day event, times vary upon an event.

COST: Free

EQUIPMENT NEEDED: Sunglasses, a camera and a lawn chair

73 DANCE OUTDOORS AT THE DTE ENERGY MUSIC THEATRE

Michigan's premier outdoor concert venue draws thousands of fans each summer to a lineup loaded with the biggest names in rock, country, and R&B music. With a capacity of more than fifteen thousand seats (including pavilion and lawn seating), the outdoor amphitheater was originally known as Pine Knob when it opened in 1972—and still is, by music lovers of a certain age. Nearly fifty years later the venue remains one of the largest amphitheaters in the United States. Since 1992 DTE Energy Music Theatre has kicked off its season on Memorial Day weekend with classic rock singer Eddie Money. He continues to make his appearance each year followed by a season that includes approximately fifty top-ranked musical acts. Expect such icons as Lady Antebellum, Dave Matthews Band, Kendrick Lamar, Nicki Minaj, Arcade Fire, Five Finger Death Punch, and Kid Rock, a hometown boy and perennial favorite among Detroit concertgoers.

7774 Sashabaw Rd., Clarkston
800-745-3000 313presents.com

KID-FRIENDLY: Yes

DOG-FRIENDLY: No

HANDICAPPED ACCESSIBLE: Limited

SEASON: Memorial Day weekend through September

HOURS: Parking lot opens at 4:30 p.m. for most evening shows and two hours prior to show start for matinees

COST: Varies

EQUIPMENT NEEDED: Comfortable shoes and a party attitude

SPECIAL COMMENTS: Guests are allowed to tailgate/picnic before events; visit website for entrance policy.

74 LOAD UP ON PRODUCE AT WESTVIEW ORCHARDS

There's one reason after another—or rather, one fruit after another—to keep visitors returning to this historic farm founded in 1813 by a veteran of the War of 1812. The farm's harvest begins in late April with the asparagus crop, followed soon after by strawberries. Once the strawberries fade, Westview's cherries take their place until the peaches, apples, pears, and pumpkins arrive in succession. Visitors can pick their own fruit or visit Westview's Farm Market, open daily from May through December. Other treats at Westview render the orchard worthy of several hours of your time. Families enjoy visiting the restored 1869 schoolhouse, the goats and calves in the petting zoo, and farm tours by tractor-driven wagon. Adults sample house-made fruit wines, and the orchard's homemade baked goods, particularly their donuts, are popular with all ages. Autumn is an especially fun time to visit: Pick your own apples, find your way through a pumpkin maze and over a straw mountain, visit the petting zoo, and snack on house-baked donuts and fall's best beverage: fresh-pressed cider.

65075 Van Dyke Rd., Washington
586-752-3123 westvieworchards.com

KID-FRIENDLY: Yes

DOG-FRIENDLY: Yes, on a leash

HANDICAPPED ACCESSIBLE: Limited

SEASON: Winery, year-round; Farm market, spring through autumn

HOURS: Farm market: daily, 8:00 a.m. to 6:00 p.m.; winery: Thurs.–Fri. 5:00–9:00 p.m., Sat. 1:00–10:00 p.m., Sun. 1:00–6:00 p.m.

COST: Free

EQUIPMENT NEEDED: Your wallet and a shopping bag

75 GET YOUR GROOVE ON AT MEADOW BROOK AMPHITHEATRE

Each summer music fans gather to hear live music under the stars at Meadow Brook, an outdoor amphitheater on the campus of Oakland University in Detroit's northern suburbs. This scenic piece of property originally belonged to automotive innovator and manufacturer John Dodge. In fact, extravagant Meadow Brook Hall, the 88,000-square-foot mansion built in 1926 by Dodge's widow, Matilda, sits just behind the trees on Estate Drive. In 1964 Dodge's family gave a portion of the estate's land to the university as an outdoor venue for the Detroit Symphony Orchestra's summertime concerts. In 1968 the performance schedule expanded to include ballet, and by the early '70s rock 'n' roll and R&B had made their way onto the Meadow Brook calendar. The DSO still performs regularly at Meadow Brook, but you can expect a wide variety of performers all season long, from Tony Bennett and Roger Daltrey to Khalid and Lady Gaga.

Oakland University, 160 Festival Dr., Rochester Hills
800-745-3000, 313presents.com

KID-FRIENDLY: Varies with concert

DOG-FRIENDLY: No

HANDICAPPED ACCESSIBLE: Limited

SEASON: April through September

HOURS: Parking lot opens at 5:30 p.m. for most evening shows and two hours prior to show start for matinees

COST: Varies

EQUIPMENT NEEDED: Comfortable shoes and a party attitude

SPECIAL COMMENTS: Guests are allowed to tailgate/picnic before events; visit website for entrance policy.

76 EAT YOUR WAY THROUGH EASTERN MARKET

Since 1841 Detroiters have been buying their produce, meat, and cut flowers at Eastern Market, making this one of the oldest farmers markets in the United States. It's easy to spend a whole morning strolling through Eastern Market's six sheds, which sprawl across four and a half acres and several city blocks near the heart of downtown. Each building shelters booths loaded with fresh meat and fish, honey, preserves, and baked goods as well as locally grown fruits and veggies, some of the items arriving from Detroit's suburbs and others grown right here in the city, in urban gardens that popped up where abandoned buildings once stood. The Saturday Market is held year-round with additional market days in the warm weather months. Not in town on market day? You can find plenty of small produce shops, butchers, bakeries, and the like open in this neighborhood every day on the streets that border the edges of Eastern Market.

2934 Russell St., Detroit
easternmarket.com

KID-FRIENDLY: Yes

DOG-FRIENDLY: No

HANDICAPPED ACCESSIBLE: Yes

SEASON: Year-round

HOURS: Saturday market 6:00 a.m. to 4:00 p.m.

COST: Free

EQUIPMENT NEEDED: Your wallet and a shopping basket

SPECIAL COMMENTS: Additional hours vary throughout the week. Wholesale market is open to public but must purchase in bulk.

77 EXPERIENCE AUTOMOTIVE HERITAGE AT AUTOPALOOZA

Beginning in late spring, all of metro Detroit celebrates its love affair with the automobile at Autopalooza, and many of the car-themed activities offer opportunities to get outside and enjoy the outdoors. Autopalooza represents a collection of at least a dozen automotive events centered on Detroit and reaching out across southeast Michigan. The summer-long party typically kicks off with the Chevrolet Detroit Grand Prix IndyCar, sports car, and super truck races on Belle Isle around Memorial Day weekend. Other events include the NASCAR races at the Michigan International Speedway; the high-end vintage auto show Concours d'Elegance, geared for those interested in both seeing and buying rare antique vehicles; and the Old Car Festival at Dearborn's Greenfield Village featuring models built between 1890 and 1932 on grounds once owned by Henry Ford himself. There's even an Orphan Car Show in mid-September, focused on long-forgotten brands, such as the DeSoto, Packard, and Willys. Among the most popular Autopalooza events is the famous Woodward Dream Cruise held annually in August.

autopalooza.org

KID-FRIENDLY: Yes

DOG-FRIENDLY: Varies with event

HANDICAPPED ACCESSIBLE: Varies with event

SEASON: April or May through mid-September

HOURS: Depends on event

COST: Depends on event

EQUIPMENT NEEDED: Sunglasses and a camera

78 BICYCLE THROUGH DETROIT HISTORY WITH MOTOR CITY BREW TOURS

One part education, one part outdoor recreation, and one part social hour, Motor City Brew Tours take suds-loving visitors on a journey through Detroit history, stopping for an adult beverage break here and there. Choose your activity level: you can take it easy and tour by bus or work up a little sweat traveling on foot or by bicycle. Tours follow such themes as The Rise and Fall of the Purple Gang, Automotive History, Murals and Public Art in Detroit, the History of Corktown and Mexicantown, and even Church History in Detroit. Pickup points and destinations range from excursions within the city proper to tours of Royal Oak, Grosse Pointe, or Belle Isle, with excursions lasting approximately three and a half hours and spanning nine to fifteen miles over paved roads. Whatever your destination or transportation of choice, the tours include stops and beer samples at three locally owned breweries, a full lunch, and ample supplies of snacks and water along the way.

248-825-3085 motorcitybrewtours.com

KID-FRIENDLY: No

DOG-FRIENDLY: No

HANDICAPPED ACCESSIBLE: No

SEASON: Bus tours, year-round; bike tours, May through September

HOURS: 9:00 a.m. to 5:00 p.m.

COST: $10 to $35

EQUIPMENT NEEDED: Sunglasses and a sense of adventure

79 STROLL THROUGH MID-CENTURY DETROIT WITH MIES VAN DER ROHE

Art deco architecture gets all the attention in the heart of Detroit, but mid-century buildings abound in The D. In the early 1950s, the world's architectural giants collaborated on the design of a large postwar housing development, a modernist community that would be called Lafayette Park. An astonishing 250 mid-century modern homes resulted from those efforts, with a remarkable 186 of the park's homes designed by the mid-century mastermind Ludwig Mies van der Rohe, who also designed Lafayette Park's three apartment towers, its elementary school, a retail district, and a thirteen-acre park called Lafayette Plaisance. The neighborhood today, which received recognition in 2015 as a National Historic Landmark by the National Park Service, represents the largest collection of Mies van der Rohe buildings in the world. Visitors can learn more about the famous architect and his life's work on free two-hour Mies-themed walking tours with the Detroit Experience Factory. Or visit the Mies Detroit website for details to plan a self-guided visit.

313-962-4590
detroitexperiencefactory.org miesdetroit.org

KID-FRIENDLY: Yes

DOG-FRIENDLY: Yes, on a leash

HANDICAPPED ACCESSIBLE: Limited

SEASON: Year-round

HOURS: Varies

COST: Free

EQUIPMENT NEEDED: Camera

80 ADMIRE THE PUBLIC ART AT HART PLAZA

All of Detroit—and a fair number of visitors—meet at downtown's Hart Plaza. Set on the banks of the Detroit River, this is the site where it's believed Antoine de la Mothe Cadillac, the French explorer and founder of Detroit, first landed in 1701. The modern plaza, which spans fourteen acres, sits at the heart of the Detroit RiverWalk and draws a great deal of attention for its public art—the circular steel *Horace E. Dodge and Son Memorial Fountain* and *Pylon* by Isamu Noguchi; the *Gateway to Freedom International Memorial to the Underground Railroad*; and *Transcending*, a monument to the Michigan labor movement. Along the park's northern edge, in the median of Woodward and Jefferson Avenues, is the famous *Monument to Joe Louis*, colloquially known as *The Fist*, an homage to the Detroit boxer. Spacious Hart Plaza can accommodate as many as forty thousand people and often does for internationally recognized events, such as the Detroit Jazz Festival, the Movement Electronic Music Festival, and the Detroit Fireworks.

1 Hart Plaza, Detroit
313-877-8057 detroitmi.gov

KID-FRIENDLY: Yes
DOG-FRIENDLY: Yes, on a leash
HANDICAPPED ACCESSIBLE: Yes

SEASON: Year-round
HOURS: Daily
COST: Free
EQUIPMENT NEEDED: Camera

81 ATTEND A FESTIVAL AT HART PLAZA

Hart Plaza forms downtown Detroit's meeting place for a summer's worth of cultural festivals. Believed by historians to be the location where French explorer Antoine de la Mothe Cadillac first set foot in Detroit in 1701, Hart Plaza spans fourteen acres and can accommodate as many as forty thousand people. You'll see that many in attendance at the city's internationally recognized Detroit Jazz Festival or the Movement Electronic Music Festival, but a host of smaller outdoor celebrations offer opportunities to experience Detroit's amazingly diverse culture firsthand. The Albanian American Festival revolves around music, dance, and food each June. North America's largest Arab and Chaldean Festival follows in July, and the Motor City Muscle rock 'n' roll 'n' muscle car festival follows in August. Arrive early to check out Hart Plaza's noteworthy public art: the circular concrete *Transcending*, honoring the labor movement; a memorial to the Underground Railroad; and, along the park's northern edge, the *Monument to Joe Louis*, known locally as *The Fist*, an homage to the Detroit boxer.

1 Hart Plaza, Detroit
313-877-8057 detroitmi.gov

KID-FRIENDLY: Yes

DOG-FRIENDLY: No

HANDICAPPED ACCESSIBLE: Limited

SEASON: May through October

HOURS: Plaza open 24 hours, festival hours vary per event

COST: Varies per event

EQUIPMENT NEEDED: Comfortable shoes and a tolerance for crowds

Photo courtesy of Amy S. Eckert

FUN AND GAMES

82 ENJOY VINTAGE BASE BALL WITH THE LAH-DE-DAHS

In 1867, Detroit hosted the first-ever World Tournament of Base Ball (spelled with two words back in those days), bringing together teams of amateur players interested in entertainment, gentlemanly recreation and exercise. Vintage base ball enthusiasts recreate that tradition at Dearborn's Greenfield Village each summer. The home team Greenfield Village Lah-De-Dahs host vintage ball clubs from around the Midwest to a weekend afternoon of base ball following 1867 rules, complete with vintage uniforms. Permissible are underhand pitching and the limited use of ball gloves (although gloves are frowned upon). Strictly prohibited is ungentlemanly behavior, to include profanity. Spectators at these vintage games sit in the grass or in lawn chairs and enjoy live period music and food along with the game. Visit in mid-August for the annual two-day World Tournament of Historic Base Ball, a commemoration of the original competition. Attendance is free with the purchase of a Greenfield Village ticket.

20900 Oakwood Blvd., Dearborn 48124
313-982-6001 thehenryford.org

KID-FRIENDLY: Yes

DOG-FRIENDLY: No

HANDICAPPED ACCESSIBLE: Yes

SEASON: June through August

HOURS: Varies, but generally 1:30 p.m. Saturdays and Sundays

COST: Free with the purchase of a Greenfield Village ticket

EQUIPMENT NEEDED: A lawn chair

83 SHARPEN YOUR GAME AT COMERICA PARK

Most people go to Comerica Park, home of the Detroit Tigers, to watch the pros in action, but since the gates open ninety minutes before the first pitch, why not work on your own baseball skills? Batting cages in the ballpark's concourse allow fans young and old to improve their pitch accuracy and speed, and throughout the season, the Tigers offer pregame, on-field baseball clinics to young players age fourteen and under. The Tigers go a step further at locations across Detroit, offering clinics for both baseball coaches and young players through a program called Play Baseball Detroit. The fun at Comerica isn't limited to baseball. Fans of all ages can catch a ride on the Fly Ball Ferris Wheel, with little cars resembling baseballs, as well as the Tiger Carousel, outfitted with tigers in place of more traditional horses, on game days, and the Walk of Fame details the club's history all the way back to the 1880s through historical exhibits.

2100 Woodward Ave., Detroit
866-66-TIGER tigers.com

KID-FRIENDLY: Yes

DOG-FRIENDLY: No

HANDICAPPED ACCESSIBLE: Yes

SEASON: April through September

HOURS: Varies

COST: Varies

EQUIPMENT NEEDED: Good running shoes, a ball cap, and a catcher's glove

SPECIAL COMMENTS: On-field pregame clinics are available for young kids and young kid teams, cost is price of ticket and $1–$2 for batting.

84 PLAY BALL WITH FIDO AT THE DETROIT DOG PARK

Long a dream of Detroit's dog lovers, the city's first dedicated dog park opened in 2014 in the heart of the city's historic Corktown neighborhood. A donation from the pet supply chain PetSmart made the PetSmart P.U.P. Detroit Dog Park a reality, a greenspace constructed on what was formerly the Macomb Playlot at 17th and Rose Streets. Located near the base of one of Corktown's most impressive and famous landmarks, the massive, empty shell of the yet-to-be-restored Michigan Central Station, the old playground seemed the perfect location for a new one—albeit geared toward pups. A double gate provides a safe, escape-proof entrance to the fenced-in park, where dogs of all breeds and sizes may run leash free (there are no separate small and large dog areas). Park benches and waste bags are provided, but plans to add a shelter and water are still in the works. The Detroit Dog Park is free and open to all, but visiting dogs must be vaccinated.

2301 17th St., Detroit
detroitdogpark.org

KID-FRIENDLY: Yes
DOG-FRIENDLY: Yes
HANDICAPPED ACCESSIBLE: Yes
SEASON: Year-round

HOURS: 7:00 a.m. to 10:00 p.m.
COST: Free
EQUIPMENT NEEDED: Fido and a frisbee

85 EMBRACE THE COLD AT THE WINTER BLAST

Winters can be long in Detroit, but the city makes the most of the snow and cold at the annual Winter Blast. Located at downtown's Campus Martius Park and surrounded by a million tiny white lights—lights that remain in the trees after brightening downtown during the holiday season—the Winter Blast brings families together for a variety of outdoor activities. Events range from free ice-skating on Campus Martius Ice Rink and an Ice Garden of lighted ice sculptures to thirty-foot slides and a zip line that whisks riders thirty-four feet over the street. A trucked-in mountain of snow allows urban dwellers to try snowboarding and skiing, and for the truly hearty, the Special Olympics Polar Plunge takes place during the Winter Blast, an opportunity to do good while having fun. If temps get to be a bit much, visitors can dig into hot fried chicken or pit-smoked BBQ at one of a dozen food trucks or warm up around the campfire roasting marshmallows for s'mores.

winterblast.com

KID-FRIENDLY: Yes

DOG-FRIENDLY: No

HANDICAPPED ACCESSIBLE: Yes

SEASON: January

HOURS: Varies for events

COST: $3, proceeds donated to charity (the recipient of these funds changes year to year), children under 3 are free.

EQUIPMENT NEEDED: Warm clothing

SPECIAL COMMENTS: After 5:00 p.m., guest under 18 must be accompanied by a parent or guardian at all times.

86 PLAY ALL DAY AT TATTAN PARK

An amazing ten acres of playground fun awaits children at Tattan Park in the western Detroit suburb of Westland. A giant twenty-thousand-square-foot play structure called the Play Planet ranks among the best jungle gyms in metro Detroit—and one of the largest in the nation—a rocket ship–themed playground with a virtual maze of slides and climbing walls, observation decks, bridges, and ramps open for fun year-round. Tattan Park is also home to the Concrete Jungle, a seventeen-thousand-square-foot skate park with a large half-pipe, three bowls, and numerous ramps. In warm weather months, the park's newest addition, the H2O Zone, offers a ridiculously fun way of cooling off, with water jets, a giant water bucket, a spitting sea serpent, and an eighteen-foot helicopter that rises ten feet above the ground and shoots water from its spinning rotors. Tattan Park also offers grilling and picnic areas, paved walking and hiking trails, and a concession area. Good luck getting the kids to leave.

1901 N. Carlson St., Westland
734-722-7620 cityofwestland.com

KID-FRIENDLY: Yes

DOG-FRIENDLY: Yes, on a leash

HANDICAPPED ACCESSIBLE: Yes

SEASON: Play Planet and Concrete Jungle, year-round; H20 Zone, Memorial Day to Labor Day

HOURS: Dawn to dusk; H20 Zone open 11:00 a.m. to 8:00 p.m.

COST: Free

EQUIPMENT NEEDED: Swimming gear, in case you want to splash in the water

87 LACE UP YOUR SKATES AT THE CAMPUS MARTIUS ICE RINK

When the snow flies, downtown's Campus Martius Park transforms its lush, green north lawn into a wintertime recreation center. Surrounded by gleaming office towers, trees covered in a million glistening white lights, and, at holiday season, backed by the city's multicolored Christmas tree and its twenty-six-foot-high menorah, Detroit's Campus Martius Ice Rink is among the city's most popular downtown outdoor recreation facilities. The rink draws crowds when it hosts performances by professional- and Olympic-caliber ice skating legends, and the Campus Martius Ice Rink forms the busy centerpiece to the Winter Blast festival each January, when Detroiters embrace the season with gusto, but locals enjoy strapping on their own skates to have a go around the rink themselves. A skate rental facility is available on-site throughout the winter as well as a warming tent in case Detroit's wintertime weather proves too much. The popular café Parc serves hot meals and drinks.

800 Woodward Ave., Detroit
313-962-0101 campusmartiuspark.org

KID-FRIENDLY: Yes

DOG-FRIENDLY: No

HANDICAPPED ACCESSIBLE: Limited

SEASON: November to March

HOURS: Mon.–Tues. 11:00 a.m. to 6:00 p.m., Wed.–Thurs. 11:00 a.m. to 9:00 p.m., Fri. 11:00 a.m. to midnight, Sat. 10:00 a.m. to 11:00 p.m., Sun. 12:00–8:00 p.m.

COST: Adults, $8; child (12 and under), $7; seniors, $7

EQUIPMENT NEEDED: Warm clothing

88 MAKE PAR AT NORTHVILLE HILLS GOLF CLUB

Surrounded by dense maple and white pine forest, natural wetlands, and a scattering of tiny inland lakes, Northville Hills Golf Club in western Detroit consistently receives high marks as a premier public golf course, and it's a course designed for both experienced and newbie golfers. Arnold Palmer and Ed Seay designed Northville Hills Golf Club in 2000 with wide, sprawling fairways; expansive; rolling greens, and numerous tees designed to suit a variety of playing abilities. Par is seventy-two over a course that ranges between 5,166 or 7,003 yards, depending on tee placement, over the course's eighteen holes. A variety of golf leagues play Northville Hills Golf Club each week, ranging from men's and women's to coed and junior leagues. There's also a senior weekday league. Avid players might consider a season pass for substantial discounts. Northville Hills' Junior Golf Academy is available for youth ages five to fifteen and includes both group and individual instruction.

15565 Bay Hill Dr., Northville
734-667-4653 northvillehillsgolfclub.com

KID-FRIENDLY: Yes

DOG-FRIENDLY: No

HANDICAPPED ACCESSIBLE: Limited

SEASON: April through October

HOURS: Mon.–Thurs. 7:00 a.m. to 9:00 p.m., Fri. 6:45 a.m. to 9:00 p.m., Sat.–Sun. 6:30 a.m. to 9:00 p.m.

COST: Prices vary from $25–$68

EQUIPMENT NEEDED: Golf clubs and gear

89 DOUBLE YOUR FUN AT GEORGE GEORGE MEMORIAL PARK

These thirty acres northeast of the city have long served as a place of fun and recreation for metro Detroiters, but until recent years the land was more likely to draw adults as part of the Moravian Golf Course. In 2008 local resident James George offered the land to Clinton Township in honor of his father, George George, which accounts for the park's repeating name. A remodeling of the golf course resulted in a lovely public park. Bridal parties are drawn to George George's landscape, its expansive emerald-green lawns, elegant fountains, flower beds, and graceful arching bridges forming the perfect backdrop for wedding ceremonies and photos, but children will love this park too. A large play structure provides slides, observation towers, bridges, and climbers. The grounds are home to mature hardwood trees and crisscrossed by biking and hiking paths. Picnic tables and public restrooms make it easy to spend the day.

40500 Moravian Rd., Clinton Twp.
586-286-8000 clintontownship.com

KID-FRIENDLY: Yes

DOG-FRIENDLY: Yes, on a leash

HANDICAPPED ACCESSIBLE: Yes

SEASON: Year-round

HOURS: 9:00 a.m. to 8:00 p.m.

COST: Free

EQUIPMENT NEEDED: Good walking shoes, since you may have to park some distance away

90 SHOOT SOME HOOPS AT THE SPORTS ZONE

You don't need to choose between a weekend in the city and an outdoor getaway. In the heart of downtown Detroit, you can experience both. The Quicken Loans Sports Zone offers the opportunity to work up a sweat at outdoor basketball and sand volleyball courts in the heart of the city's central business district. The courts sit directly east of Campus Martius Park in Cadillac Square, and they're open to the public all summer long. Join a league and play with other sports enthusiasts, or reserve a volleyball or basketball court yourself for an evening of fun with some friends or work colleagues. After you've shot a few hoops, you'll find plenty of places to grab a meal or a drink afterward. Check out Parc, Woodward Coney Island, Central Kitchen + Bar, or the Detroit Water Ice Factory. All are located in or near Cadillac Square and Campus Martius Park.

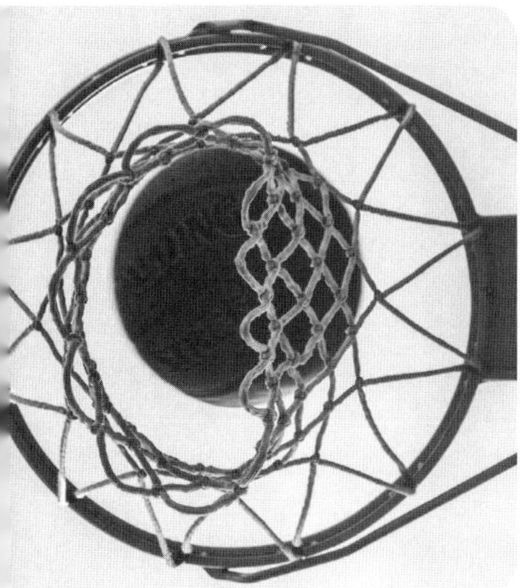

Cadillac Square, Detroit
248-845-8273 comeplaydetroit.com

KID-FRIENDLY: Yes

DOG-FRIENDLY: Yes, on a leash

HANDICAPPED ACCESSIBLE: Yes

SEASON: Memorial Day to Labor Day

HOURS: 9:00 a.m. to 9:00 p.m.

COST: Free

EQUIPMENT NEEDED: Sports gear

91 PHOTOGRAPH A MERMAID AT THE CULLEN FAMILY CAROUSEL

The colorful Cullen Family Carousel is just one of several family-oriented attractions on Rivard Plaza, part of the always-busy Detroit RiverWalk. Installed in 2007 as an early and integral part of the decade-long revitalization of the downtown waterway, the Cullen Family Carousel was designed to reflect its unique surroundings. Beneath a blue-and-white striped canopy, the carousel's decorative panels feature elaborate dragonflies and images of the Detroit River's flora and fauna. In place of traditional horses, the carousel's seats were custom sculpted to resemble local wildlife: a wide-eyed bullfrog, a flying loon, and a blue-winged heron standing tall. If the elegant bead-adorned mermaid and slithering river monster aren't exactly indigenous to the Detroit River, they are beautiful nonetheless. Other fun pastimes alongside the carousel include a map of the Detroit River inlaid in granite, a map of the St. Lawrence Seaway sculpted of glass, a children's playground, fountains, public art, and colorful flower gardens.

Rivard Plaza on the Detroit RiverWalk
1340 Atwater St., Detroit
313-566-8200 detroitriverfront.org

KID-FRIENDLY: Yes

DOG-FRIENDLY: No

HANDICAPPED ACCESSIBLE: Yes

SEASON: Memorial Day to Labor Day

HOURS: 10:00 a.m. to 8:00 p.m.

COST: $1 per person

EQUIPMENT NEEDED: Camera and comfortable shoes to explore the RiverWalk

92 CATCH A SOCCER GAME WITH THE DETROIT CITY FOOTBALL CLUB

If there's any sports team that can claim a grassroots beginning in The D, it's the Detroit City Football Club. Back in 2010, a group of five soccer die-hards looked around at the success of Detroit's coed recreational leagues while playing on the Belle Isle soccer pitch. More than a thousand players were gathering each week at clubs across metro Detroit at that time, and it seemed only natural that they tap into the sport's popularity to grow soccer to its next level. Those soccer enthusiasts have since launched the DCFC, a semipro club within the National Premier Soccer League. Games are played at Keyworth Stadium in Hamtramck, where concessions are offered by a fun assortment of food trucks, and parking is free if you arrive by bicycle. Want even more soccer? The Detroit City Futbol League continues. The DCFL offers adult coed recreational soccer neighborhood and bar leagues in partnership with the Detroit City Football Club. Visit the team's website for information.

3201 Roosevelt St., Hamtramck
313-265-3630 detcityfc.com

KID-FRIENDLY: Yes

DOG-FRIENDLY: No

HANDICAPPED ACCESSIBLE: Yes

SEASON: April through July

HOURS: Varies

COST: Single ticket $25

EQUIPMENT NEEDED: Comfortable shoes and a camera

93 SPLASH AWAY THE DAY AT MT. ELLIOTT PARK

Along the 3.5-mile length of the Detroit Riverfront that's been transformed into the Detroit RiverWalk, Mt. Elliott Park and Pavilion may rank as the child friendliest of them all. Located just west of the Douglas MacArthur Bridge to Belle Isle, this stretch of land was an eyesore just a few years ago, the pier crumbling with age and neglect and the landscape occupied by parking lots, but a massive investment in riverfront improvement converted Mt. Elliott Park into a Great Lakes schooner-themed spray park custom-made for a hot day in the city. The schooner's masts spout sheets of water. Geysers shoot out of the pavement, and child-powered water cannons squirt from near the ship's steering wheel. Expansive green lawns and attractive winding pathways also make the park a good spot for pushing a stroller or throwing around a Frisbee. Pleasant patio tables and chairs sit outside the adjacent RiverWalk Café, which serves snacks and drinks in warm weather.

110 Mt. Elliott St., Detroit
313-566-8200 detroitriverfront.org

KID-FRIENDLY: Yes

DOG-FRIENDLY: Yes, on a leash

HANDICAPPED ACCESSIBLE: Yes

SEASON: Memorial Day to Labor Day

HOURS: 6 a.m. to 10:00 p.m.

COST: Free

EQUIPMENT NEEDED: Swimming gear if you plan to get wet

94 BUILD A SANDCASTLE AT CAMPUS MARTIUS PARK

Way back in 1788, Detroit's military recruits trained at the city's Campus Martius, which in Latin means "military ground." More than two centuries later, this 2.5-acre public square in downtown Detroit serves as the city's gathering space. Surrounded by glass-and-steel office towers, shops, and restaurants, Campus Martius Park provides a small green respite for employees looking for a little fresh air at lunchtime. The park also serves as a popular urban playground for families. In summer, the park transforms into a spectacular beach with dump trucks full of golden beach sand. Relax in a lounge chair under a colorful umbrella. Sink your toes into the warm sand, and let the children have fun with the beach buckets and shovels there for public use. In winter, Campus Martius opens its public ice rink. Year-round there's a fountain, live music, a tidy lawn, colorful landscaping, patio tables, food trucks, and the popular bistro Parc.

800 Woodward Ave., Detroit
313-962-0101 campusmartiuspark.org

KID-FRIENDLY: Yes

DOG-FRIENDLY: Yes, on a leash

HANDICAPPED ACCESSIBLE: Yes

SEASON: Year-round

HOURS: 24 hours

COST: Free

EQUIPMENT NEEDED: Sunblock and sand toys

95 RUN FORD FIELD WITH THE DETROIT LIONS

Ford Field, home to the Detroit Lions, sits at the heart of one of North America's premier sports destinations. The NFL stadium is located just blocks away from Comerica Park, where the Detroit Tigers play, and Little Caesars Arena, which became home to the Red Wings and the Pistons in 2017. While the Lions rank as one of only a handful of teams never to have played in the Super Bowl, Detroiters are nothing if not loyal fans. Each fall fans fill the sixty-five-thousand-seat stadium hoping for a winning season, and after most home games children are invited to see for themselves how it feels to run the length of the Lions' football field. Register children online to participate in the Kids' Touchdown Run and become eligible for prizes. If that's not enough football for you, check out the Lions' football camps. They're held each summer across metro Detroit and around the state.

2000 Brush St., Detroit
313-262-2000 fordfield.com

KID-FRIENDLY: Kids' Touchdown Run, ages 5–14; youth camps, ages 6–18

DOG-FRIENDLY: No

HANDICAPPED ACCESSIBLE: No

SEASON: Football camps, summer; touchdown run, fall and winter

HOURS: Monday through Friday 10:00 a.m. to 6:00 p.m.

COST: Varies per game

EQUIPMENT NEEDED: Good running shoes

96 INTRODUCE YOUR FUZZY FRIEND TO SHINOLA

Once a revitalized Midtown became the popular place for young creative types to live, work, shop, and dine, it was only a matter of time before the neighborhood would need a proper dog park. Local manufacturer and trendy watch- and bicycle-maker Shinola—which also happens to sell a line of pet accessories—came to the rescue, helping to fund the park's construction. The Midtown Detroit Dog Park is small, but it allows dogs of all sizes to run off leash in a safe, fenced-in space, and there's a picnic table where human visitors can rest their feet. The park sits in close proximity to Midtown's most popular hot spots, including Jolly Pumpkin Artisan Ales, Third Man Records, Cass Corridog, a dog- and cat-friendly pet boutique, and, naturally, Shinola's flagship Detroit store. You'll recognize the Midtown Detroit Dog Park when you see it. There's a shiny chrome Shinola clock towering over the lawn.

Cass Ave. at W. Canfield St., Detroit
midtowndetroitinc.org

KID-FRIENDLY: Yes
DOG-FRIENDLY: Yes
HANDICAPPED ACCESSIBLE: Yes
SEASON: Year-round

HOURS: 7:00 a.m. to 8:30 p.m.
COST: Free
EQUIPMENT NEEDED: Fuzzy and a frisbee

97 LEARN ABOUT CRICKET WITH THE DETROIT CRICKET LEAGUE

In the 1850s, cricket reigned as Detroit's most popular sport. By far. Detroiters enjoyed the sport at the Peninsular Cricket Club, on a broad grassy field now occupied by the restaurants and bars of the trendy Midtown neighborhood. While baseball soon stole Americans' interest away from cricket, you'll find plenty of enthusiasts in metro Detroit thanks in large part to the presence of immigrants from cricket-loving nations, India and Pakistan among them. The game is played on a circular field between two teams of eleven players each and remains the world's second most-popular game after soccer. Games are notorious for lasting a good long time, but it's worth checking out this sport, which remains popular in The D. Local matches take place across Detroit between such teams as the Indus Thunders from Farmington Hills; the Hawks from Troy; the Super Kings from Southfield; and the Gladiators, Cruisers, and Rising Stars from the city of Detroit. Visit the Detroit Cricket League's website for a listing of matches across southeastern Detroit.

detroitcricketleague.org

KID-FRIENDLY: Yes

DOG-FRIENDLY: No

HANDICAPPED ACCESSIBLE: Varies with field

SEASON: May through October

HOURS: Saturday and Sunday

COST:

EQUIPMENT NEEDED: Sunglasses and patience—cricket games have a reputation for being long

98 TEE OFF AT SHEPHERD'S HOLLOW GOLF CLUB

This lush 350-acre golf course in northwest Detroit was built on land formerly operated as the Colombiere Center, a retreat once used by the Detroit Province of the Society of Jesus, a Catholic order of priests. With its gently rolling hills, sparkling lakes, meticulously landscaped grounds, and mature hardwood trees, Shepherd's Hollow comes about as close to golfing heaven as you're likely to find in metro Detroit. Directional bunkers characterize the long, narrow, tree- and lake-bordered fairways. Par is seventy-two over 7,236 yards for the course's first eighteen holes, and if that's not enough, play another nine: Shepherd's Hollow offers twenty-seven. After your game, linger over dinner at Shepherd's Hollow's white, colonnaded restaurant. Dine inside by the fireplace when the weather grows cool. In warmer weather, celebrate Detroit's short summers out on the terrace to feast on a meal created with produce grown right in the resort's own gardens.

9085 Big Lake Rd., Clarkston
248-922-0300 shepherdshollow.com

KID-FRIENDLY: No
DOG-FRIENDLY: No
HANDICAPPED ACCESSIBLE: Limited
SEASON: April through October
HOURS: 6:30 a.m. to 9:00 p.m.
COST: $49 to $85
EQUIPMENT NEEDED: Golf clubs and gear

99 RELAX AT BOOTH PARK

Booth Park sits on land that originally housed an inter-urban railway station. After the railway closed, the Booth family, of newspaper fame, purchased the property and donated it to the city of Birmingham. It was in 2007 that residents teamed up to pay for, plan, and build the play structures in today's Booth Park. The park's wooden playground entertains children for hours. Twenty thousand square feet of space includes a tower modeled after Birmingham's old fire station. There are extensive interconnecting bridges, slides and swings, tunnels and observation decks, and a spinning wheel that sprays a mist of water. The park's amphitheater occasionally hosts live music performances, and the nearby hill is not only fun for wintertime tobogganing, but it's also covered with artificial turf, making it possible to slide down the hill year-round. Beautiful landscaping and umbrella tables make it a nice spot for an afternoon picnic too. A footpath joins Booth Park to the Rouge River Trail, a route perfect for bicyclists and runners.

N. Old Woodward Ave. at Harmon St., Birmingham
248-530-1800 bhamgov.org

KID-FRIENDLY: Yes

DOG-FRIENDLY: Yes, on a leash

HANDICAPPED ACCESSIBLE: Yes

SEASON: Year-round

HOURS: Office hours 8:00 a.m. to 5:00 p.m.

COST: Free

EQUIPMENT NEEDED: Your wallet, so you can pop into Birmingham's shops afterward

SPECIAL COMMENTS: Booth park has a Little Free Library housed inside a brightly painted pig. It's a "take a book, leave a book" free book exchange.

100 PLAY BALL AT THE CORNER BALLPARK

The Corner Ballpark is new, but its history is long and storied. For more than a century, the Detroit Tigers (and the Detroit Lions from 1938 to 1974) played on this chunk of land at the corner of Michigan Avenue and Trumbull Street in Corktown. The team abandoned Tiger Stadium in 2000 in favor of the newly built Comerica Park downtown. For years Detroiters expected the old Tiger Stadium lot to be redeveloped into businesses or condos, but an impassioned few fought for a different vision, and in 2018 the Detroit Police Athletic League unveiled the culmination of that dream, a five-year, $21 million project called the Corner Ballpark. The park allows PAL youth to continue a baseball tradition on the very ground where such legendary athletes as Hank Greenberg, Al Kaline, Ty Cobb, Willie Horton, and Mickey Lolich made sports history. PAL offers opportunities for fourteen thousand youth to become engaged in sports, robotics, and other enrichment programs across metro Detroit. To register for programs or attend a sporting event, visit PAL's website.

Michigan Avenue at Trumbull Street
313-833-1600 detroitpal.org

KID-FRIENDLY: Yes

DOG-FRIENDLY: No

HANDICAPPED ACCESSIBLE: Yes

SEASON: April through September

HOURS: Varies per event

COST: Free

EQUIPMENT NEEDED: Camera and a sense of nostalgia

Photo courtesy of Amy S. Eckert

PHOTO CREDITS

1. Learn to Row with the Nation's Oldest Rowing Club—Photo courtesy of Flickr
2. Cruise the Detroit River with *Diamond Jack*—Photo courtesy of Diamond Jack's River Tours
3. Invent a New Fish Tale at Bishop Park—Photo courtesy of City of Wyandotte
4. Take the Plunge for Special Olympics—Photo courtesy of Special Olympics Michigan
5. Learn to Sail on Lake St. Clair—Photo courtesy of Pixabay
6. Take a Dip in the Detroit River—Photo courtesy of Pixabay
7. Cruise in Style aboard the *Infinity* and *Ovation*—Photo courtesy of Infinity and Ovation Yacht Charters
8. Set Sail for Canada aboard the *Detroit Princess*—Photo courtesy of Amy S. Eckert
9. Explore Detroit's Waterways with SUP—Photo (page 12) courtesy of Pixabay, photo (page 13) courtesy of Riverside Kayak Connection
10. Fish for Bass, Walleye, and Muskie with a Fishing Charter—Photos courtesy of Pixabay
11. Discover Historic Canals with Riverside Kayak Connection—Photo courtesy of Riverside Kayak Connection
12. Explore Lake St. Clair with the Detroit Outpost—Photo courtesy of Amy S. Eckert
13. Cool Off with a Swim at Lake St. Clair—Photo courtesy of Flickr
14. Paddle around Belle Isle—Photo courtesy of Amy S. Eckert
15. Paddle to Dinner with Detroit River Sports—Photo courtesy of Amy S. Eckert
16. Combine Cruising with Beer Tasting on a Motor City Brew Tour—Photo courtesy of Amy S. Eckert
17. Pedal and Party on a Detroit Cycle Boat—Photo courtesy of Nicholas and Jody Blazczyk: Owners of Detroit Cycle Boat
18. Learn to Kayak with the Riverside Kayak Connection—Photo courtesy of Amy S. Eckert
19. Pedal The D at Slow Roll—Photo courtesy of Tour de Troit
20. Go Snowboarding at Alpine Valley—Photo courtesy of Pixabay
21. Enjoy Yoga on the Detroit River—Photo courtesy of Detroit Riverfront Conservancy
22. Cycle the City with Wheelhouse Detroit—Photo courtesy of Amy S. Eckert
23. Run along the Detroit RiverWalk—Photo courtesy of Detroit Riverfront Conservancy
24. Walk through History at Greenfield Village—Photo courtesy of Greenfield Village
25. Bicycle to Eastern Market by the Graffiti-Rich Dequindre Cut Greenway—Photo courtesy of Detroit Riverfront Conservancy
26. Explore Architecture with Preservation Detroit—Photo courtesy of Amy S. Eckert
27. Run the Turkey Trot at America's Thanksgiving Parade—Photo courtesy of Karen Elliott

28. Bicycle Belle Isle State Park—Photo courtesy of Amy S. Eckert
29. Learn to Camp, Fish, and Hunt Downtown at the Outdoor Adventure Center—Photo courtesy of Amy S. Eckert
30. Cruise Detroit by Segway—Photo courtesy of Flickr
31. Take a Hike (or a Bike) along the Iron Belle Trail—Photo courtesy of Detroit Riverfront Conservancy
32. See the Motor City Sans Motor with Tour de Troit—Photo courtesy of Tour de Troit
33. Explore Abandoned Detroit on a Motor City Photography Tour—Photo courtesy of Amy S. Eckert
34. Tour Downtown by the QLine—Photo courtesy of Amy S. Eckert
35. Pedal American-Made Wheels at Detroit Bikes—Photo courtesy of Detroit Bikes
36. Admire Detroit's Marble Lighthouse— Photo courtesy of Amy S. Eckert
37. Run to Canada (and Back Again) at the Detroit Marathon—Photo courtesy of Detroit Riverfront Conservancy
38. Hike (or Bike) the Clinton River Trail—Photo courtesy of Amy S. Eckert
39. Rent some Wheels with MoGo Detroit—Photo courtesy of Amy S. Eckert
40. Spend Holiday Nights at Greenfield Village—Photo (page 58) courtesy of KMS Photography for Greenfield Village, photo (page 59) courtesy of Roy Ritchie for Greenfield Village
41. Go People Watching at Beacon Park—Photo courtesy of Amy S. Eckert
42. Bicycle Midtown, Outdoors and In—Photo courtesy of Detroit Bikes
43. Dig in Clara Ford's Gardens at the Henry Ford Estate Fair Lane—Photo courtesy of Amy S. Eckert
44. Tiptoe through the Tulips at the Anna Scripps Whitcomb Conservatory—Photo courtesy of Amy S. Eckert
45. Spy on Birds at Belle Isle—Photo courtesy of Pixabay
46. Chill with the Penguins at the Detroit Zoo—Photo courtesy of Amy S. Eckert
47. Release your Inner Shutterbug at Sunset Point—Photo courtesy of Amy S. Eckert
48. Enjoy the Wildflowers at William G. Milliken State Park—Photo courtesy of Amy S. Eckert
49. Feed the Deer at Belle Isle Nature Center—Photo courtesy of Amy S. Eckert
50. Stroll through the Flower Beds at Gabriel Richard Park—Photo courtesy of Ken Cobb for the Detroit Riverfront Conservancy
51. Become a Citizen Forester with the Greening of Detroit—Photos courtesy of Pixabay
52. Experience Flower Day at Eastern Market—Photo courtesy of Amy S. Eckert
53. Learn about Trees and History at Elmwood Cemetery—Photo courtesy of Amy S. Eckert
54. Stroll the Grounds of the Edsel and Eleanor Ford House—Photo courtesy of Amy S. Eckert
55. Enjoy Fall Foliage along the Paint Creek Trail—Photo courtesy of Flickr

56. See Meadow Brook in Bloom—Photo courtesy of M. J. Beznos for Meadow Brook Hall
57. Explore the Nation's Oldest Aquarium at Belle Isle—Photo courtesy of Amy S. Eckert
58. Zip through the Trees at TreeRunner Adventure Park—Photo courtesy of TreeRunner Adventure Parks
59. Tap a Maple Tree at One of Detroit's Metroparks—Photos courtesy of Flickr
60. Take a Bird-Themed Field Trip with the Detroit Audubon Society—Photos courtesy of Pixabay
61. Watch Artists at Work at Murals in the Market—Photo courtesy of Amy S. Eckert
62. Celebrate the Season at Noel Night—Photo courtesy of Flickr
63. Tour Detroit's Galleries on Second Saturdays—Photo courtesy of Wasserman Projects, artwork credit, Markus Linnenbrink + Nick Gelpi "THEFIRSTONEISCRAZYTHESECONDONEISNUTS" 2015, photo credit: Everest Guerra
64. Discover the World of Jazz at the Detroit Jazz Festival—Photo courtesy of Flickr
65. Pedal for Your Drinks with the HandleBar—Photo courtesy of HandleBar Detroit
66. See Detroit's Cityscape with Detroit Urban Adventures—Photo courtesy of Amy S. Eckert
67. Witness the Comeback City with the Detroit Experience Factory—Courtesy Amy S. Eckert
68. Explore the Outdoor Sculptures at Cranbrook Academy of Art—Photo courtesy of Amy S. Eckert
69. Feel the Energy at Movement Electronic Music Festival—Photo courtesy of Brandon Nagy, Flickr
70. Discover Public Art in the People Mover—Photo courtesy of Amy S. Eckert
71. Cycle Urban Gardens with Wheelhouse Detroit—Photo courtesy of Wheelhouse Detroit
72. Check Out the Rides at the Woodward Dream Cruise—Photo courtesy of Pixabay
73. Dance Outdoors at the DTE Energy Music Theatre—Photo courtesy of Flickr
74. Load Up on Produce at Westview Orchards—Photo (page 128) courtesy of Pixabay, photo (page 129) courtesy of Amy S. Eckert
75. Get Your Groove on at Meadow Brook Amphitheater—Photo courtesy of Flickr
76. Eat Your Way through Eastern Market—Photo courtesy of Amy S. Eckert
77. Experience Automotive Heritage at Autopalooza—Photo courtesy of Allen Best, Flickr
78. Bicycle through Detroit History with Motor City Brew Tours—Photo courtesy of Pixaby, Amy S. Eckert
79. Stroll through Mid-Century Detroit with Mies van der Rohe—Photo courtesy of Amy S. Eckert
80. Admire the Public Art at Hart Plaza—Photo courtesy of Amy S. Eckert
81. Attend a Festival at Hart Plaza—Photo courtesy of Detroit Riverfront Conservancy

82. Enjoy Vintage Base Ball with the Lah-De-Dahs—Photo courtesy of Henry Ford Museum
83. Sharpen Your Game at Comerica Park—Photo courtesy of Amy S. Eckert
84. Play Ball with Fido at the Detroit Dog Park—Photo courtesy of Pixabay
85. Embrace the Cold at the Winter Blast—Photo courtesy of Flickr
86. Play All Day at Tattan Park—Photo courtesy of Amy S. Eckert
87. Lace up Your Skates at the Campus Martius Ice Rink—Photo courtesy of Pixabay
88. Make Par at Northville Hills Golf Club—Photo courtesy of Pixaby
89. Double Your Fun at George George Memorial Park—Photo courtesy of Amy S. Eckert
90. Shoot Some Hoops at the Sports Zone—Photo courtesy of Pixabay
91. Photograph a Mermaid at the Cullen Family Carousel—Photo courtesy of Diana Lambdin Meyer
92. Catch a Soccer Game with the Detroit City Football Club—Photo courtesy of Detroit City Football Club
93. Splash Away the Day at Mt. Elliott Park—Photo courtesy of Detroit Riverfront Conservancy
94. Build a Sandcastle at Campus Martius Park—Photo courtesy of Pixabay
95. Run Ford Field with the Detroit Lions—Photo courtesy of Architectural Polymers, Flickr
96. Introduce Your Fuzzy Friend to Shinola—Photo courtesy of Pixabay
97. Learn about Cricket with the Detroit Cricket League—Photos courtesy of Pixaby
98. Tee Off at Shepherd's Hollow Golf Club—Photo courtesy of Pixaby
99. Relax at Booth Park—Photo courtesy of Amy S. Eckert
100. Play Ball at the Corner Ballpark—Photo courtesy of Amy S. Eckert

INDEX